A Fragile Union

A
Fragile
Union

New & Selected
Writings

Joan Nestle

CLEIS
PRESS

Published in the United States by Cleis Press Inc.,
P.O. Box 14684, San Francisco, California 94114.

Printed in the United States.
Cover design: Karen Huff
Cover photograph: Kathryn Kirk
Text design: Ned Takahashi
Logo art: Juana Alicia
First Edition.
10 9 8 7 6 5 4 3 2 1

Library of Congress Cataloging-in-Publication Data

Nestle Joan, 1940-
    A Fragile Union: new & selected writings / Joan Nestle.
        p.   cm.
    Includes bibliographical references (p. 206)
    ISBN 1 - 57344 - 040 - X (alk. paper)
    1. Joan Nestle,   1940-   .   2. Women authors, American–20th
century–biography.   3. Cancer–Patients–United States–Biography.
4. Women teachers–United States–Biography.   5. Autobiographical
fiction, American.   6. Lesbians–United States–Biography.
7. Lesbians–Fiction.   I.   Title
PS3564.E822F73   1998
818'.5409 – dc21   98 - 31261
                                                                                          CIP

"A Feeling Comes" first appeared in *Lesbian Love Stories,* vol. 2, ed. Irene Zahava, Freedom, CA: The Crossing Press, 1991. "I Lift My Eyes to the Hill" originated as a talk given on the occasion of the first annual David A. Kessler Lecture in Lesbian and Gay Studies, CLAGS, City University of New York, November 20, 1992. An earlier version of "John Preston and Myself" appeared as the introduction to *Sister and Brother: Lesbians and Gay Men Write About Their Lives Together* (San Francisco: HarperSanFrancisco, 1994). "Leaving Home: Memories, Diversity, and Marginality" is based on a talk presented at an older women's educational forum at Bryn Mawr College in 1992. "Letter to My Community: A Sturdy Yes of a People" was first published in *Gay Community News*, 1993. An earlier version of "My Woman Poppa" first appeared in *On Our Backs* 5 (Summer 1988) and was reprinted in *Lesbian Love Stories*, vol. 1, ed. Irene Zahava, Freedom, CA: The Crossing Press, 1989. An earlier version of "Narratives of Liberation: Pluralities of Hope" was presented as a speech to a group of teachers, students, and administrators at the University of Kansas, October 1994. An early version of "Regina at the Races" first appeared in *A Restricted Country*, Ithaca: Firebrand Books, 1987. "The Uses of Strength" first appeared in *Heatwave: Women in Love and Lust: Lesbian Short Fiction*, ed. Lucy Jane Bledsoe, Los Angeles: Alyson Publications, 1995. An earlier version of "The Will to Remember: The Lesbian Herstory Archives" appeared in the *Feminist Review* 34 (Spring 1990). An early version of "Woman of Muscle, Woman of Bone" appeared in *Bad Attitude* 6 (Summer 1990) and a revised version in *Tangled Sheets*, eds. Rosamund Elwin and Karen X. Tulchinsky, Toronto, Ontario: Women's Press, 1995.

To June Bobb,
whose friendship has never proven fragile

In Gratitude

To Sydelle Kramer of the Frances Goldin Literary Agency for her patience, perseverance, and caring.

To Lee Hudson.

To Leni Goodman; David Sumberg; Naomi Replansky; Eva Kollisch; Nancy Wilson; Karin Lützen; Linda Levine; Dawn Esposito; Marsha Labovitz; Joy Rich, Maxine Feldman; the women of the archives; Riki Anne Wilchins; Chelsea Elisabeth Goodwin and Rusty Mae Moore; Jacquie Bishop; all the women of the Black Slip celebration; Gayle Rubin; my students, all twenty-nine years of you; Phyllis Pitts; Ruth Warrantz; Liz Kennedy and Bobbi Prebis; Gerry Gomez Pearlberg; Madeline Davis and Wendy Smiley; Morgan Gwenwald; Saskia Scheffer; Kathryn Kirk; Haya Shalom; Jenifer Firestone and her daughter Hannah; Barbara Cruikshank; Namita Dwarka; Peggy Shaw; Lois Weaver; Ginu Kamani; Darian, Delores, Rachel, Yvette, and all the other women who struggle with my health insurance, take my blood, read my counts, and keep track of the IV; Dr. Bernadette Davis-Lorten; Dr. Avi Barbasch; the authors of a lifelong book of texts that have held me in the arms of their words; Jan Boney; Steven Kruger; Pat Califia; Ann Snitow; my neighbors at 215 who kept an eye on me; Maxene Kupperman-Guiñales; Deborah Edel; Karyn London; Marilyn Hacker; Emile Zola and Patrick O'Brian, whose novels were very good friends in a difficult time; Studs Terkel, whom I have never met but who took notice of my work.

To the memories of Sonny Wainwright, Pat Parker, Isaaca Siegel, Audre Lorde, and Kathleen Martindale.

To Felice Newman and Frédérique Delacoste for saying yes.

To Dianne Otto, who braves life's dangers and brings me hope.

Table of Contents

III. Our Gift of Touch

Introduction

There is no guarantee that the flowers I have chosen
would flatter the eye when assembled. Besides
there are others I can't call to mind. But there's no
hurry. I shall dig them all into their storage trenches,
some in my memory, the others in my imagination.
There, they can still find the humus, the slightly
bitter water, the warmth and the gratitude which
will perhaps keep them from dying.
– Colette

    With this book, I offer you the fragile unions that are my life–
the life of a fifty-eight-year-old white Jewish fem lesbian woman with
cancer living in New York City in the United States of America at the end
of the twentieth century. I give you these details not as markers of identity
the way we often did in the lesbian-feminist movement of the 1970s and
'80s, thinking that if we laid out our particulars, we had cleared away all
ambiguity about our lives, but precisely for the opposite reason. Each of
the listed elements represents huge worlds of shifting meaning, unending

searches for what can keep my love and what has to be let go. Nothing feels certain to me now, other than the precariousness of my under-standings and my continued need to touch. But contrary to what some have said about this legacy of doubt, I find this to be a time of great pas-sion in my life, a time of increased commitments to the forging of fragile solidarities that, if of the body, may last only a night, and if of a more sweeping kind, carry me more humbly than ever into historical processes.

My writing grows out of desperate quandaries—both personal and national. How to love when I keep failing, how to be brave when I am so fearful, how to protest injustices when I am so tired, how to embrace difference when I do not even trust myself? I am still haunted by the Reagan years, when I was so aware of the fragility of the social world around me, when I saw a country so marked by arrogance, so assaulted by national malice that I turned to my other America, one in which to be poor was not a crime and one that recognized that economic ambition without a compassionate social vision was a form of national cruelty. I found this other country in the lives of my open-enrollment students in the Queens College SEEK Program, in my lesbian-queer community, and in my own immediate world of sex and desire. In all these places I saw how fragile hope was and yet how tenaciously it survived in the lives of those who lived below the gaze of national power. In Reagan's America and still in this one, we run the risk of drowning in one another's histo-ries. When opportunities are callously diminished and the distance between those who have more than they need and those who have less grows into a class divide so wide that whole generations, in despair, plunge into it, how can we find a way back to honor one another's stories?

In my twenty-five-year history with the Lesbian Herstory Archives, I set myself the goal of commemorating the differences among lives in the hope of finding shared grounds of tenacity and tenderness. It was my search for documents of connection that inspired several essays in this collection. I do not in any way think that my friendship with Mabel Hampton, an eighty-three-year-old African American lesbian woman, mitigated the racial and economic injustices this country doled out to her, but in presenting the words of her life, I hope I have preserved for others the gift of her self-awareness and her recognition of the life-giving power of multiple communities of sustenance. The essay "My Fem Quest" grows out of an intergenerational conversation with Barbara Cruikshank, an astute young woman who experiences her desire with a different set of questions than my 1950s-created fem self ever thought to ask. I have been gifted in my later life with the friendship of several younger women whose minds glow with the challenge of deconstructing ideas into which their lives no longer fit. These friendships are fragile unions of a very special kind. I carry my past rather heavy-handedly, but these young women understand where my need for certainty comes from, while I try to ground their longings in possibilities of meaning that I have come to trust. Finally, in my writing about John Preston, my co-editor of *Sister and Brother: Lesbians and Gay Men Write About Their Lives Together* and comrade in the writing of what some call pornography, I offer the portrait of a friendship based on a mutual respect for the difficult task of erotic writing. John died of AIDS before our collaborative work was finished, but he educated me about the generosity of friends who are writers, even when they are under the deadliest of sieges.

John, in his last months, in 1994, would call me late at night to make sure I understood what final touches our book still needed and to tell me of his struggle to preserve the John Preston he had worked so hard to create; the strong, direct master of other men's erotic fantasies. What John and I did not know at that time was that I, too, was harboring a cellular battle for life that would change my days. In 1995, I was diagnosed with advanced colon cancer. Fragility now defines my body in a more profound way than ever before. The cellular surge of cancer and the late-twentieth-century medical answer of poisoning all to kill some is a permanent discourse within my skin. In some way I must work out a collaboration with the energy of this disease. Cancer cells want to be immortal—they are lovers of their own life—but for me to live, they must die. This is the crack at the center now, the primary fissure that I must find a way to allow to exist within me. Like John, I use writing about the body and my need for touch as a way to negotiate my terror and to honor life.

In the ten years encompassed by the writings in this book, I have participated in my queer communities' struggle for political, legal, and social respect. This has taken me from protests in the street over the exclusion of gay people from New York's St. Patrick's Day parade to speaking about the history of lesbian sexuality at the SUNY, New Paltz, conference on women's sexuality. In so doing, I have been reminded of the strange position gay people and lesbians now find themselves in. National messages concerning our right to a public life are contradictory: Ellen can be a TV lesbian for six months, but like a pornographic novel, she comes with a warning; gay women and men can serve in the armed forces as long as they are silent about their love while they are being trained to kill; women talking about specific sexual practices on a college campus are called "unnatural" by a *Wall Street Journal* columnist because they dare to separate sexuality from reproduction. At a time like this, cultural exchanges become a marketplace for cultural betrayals.

We live in a society that still debates almost every aspect of our lives in the daily newspapers. There, we learn which religion has decided not to allow gay marriages, which right-wing candidate has most forcefully announced that no gay person will ever serve in his administration, which state has voted to repeal its law prohibiting discrimination against gay people. These are only the most obvious examples of the problem we pose for this society. Violence against transgendered and transsexual people remains the invisible crime it always has been in this country. Many current national cultural discussions are coded angers at our presence–the rage at "postmodern" changes in the college curriculum has homophobia as one of its unspoken driving forces. Look what has happened since we let queer theory into the gates of academia–that is the subtext of repeated articles bemoaning the decadent state of late-twentieth-century literary and cultural discussions. Now, leading academic historians who once knew better are urging us to bring history back into the professional fold, away from the people who suffer its consequences. In the 1980s it was grassroots lesbian and gay scholars who showed the potential for new sources of historical knowledge and more egalitarian ways of sharing the resulting insights. In the battle over funding for the arts, we have seen a nation willing to dismantle its program of support rather than signal its acceptance of the gay imagination.

I have been lucky enough in my own life to have participated in the beginning moments of a people's movement from private history to public discourse. I remember the early meetings in Boston, Manhattan, Maine, San Francisco, and Toronto, where a handful of men and women gathered to share their discoveries and to agonize over how to find the money to continue their work, how best to share these discoveries with the communities they were documenting, and how to balance the need for anonymity–a survival tactic of our people for so long–against the delight of revelation. I remember the flickering slide shows, capturing the lost faces and communal streets of other gay times, and the stunned recognition of audiences who were meeting for the first time with their own public story. In those days, we were not always sure that this fledgling idea of lesbian and gay history would find a home in the world, and after it did, after a few years of students learning about how large communities of lesbian women lived a different American history or how American culture was influenced by a gay sensibility or how world literature is marked by the experience of same-sex love, many academicians and politicians are now decrying this "trivializing" of learning. The gay community has always been at the mercy of other people's ideas about us, whether they were medical, legal, or religious. But we will not go back into an intellectual closet. Ideas belong to no one kind of people, and while they have the power to both enslave and liberate, they are also fragile expressions of hope, hope that the most maligned can articulate their own pasts and envision their own futures.

Because I entered the culturally policed queer community in

the 1950s, my sense of the history of this struggle for liberation is long and deep; my writing is in the service of a political and cultural struggle–I am proud of that–but the other part of this admission is the responsibility I feel to create no new prisons while I try to dismantle old ones. Some of the writing in this book is a rereading of my own texts, in which I share with my readers what I now feel I got wrong the first time around; in some cases, I am not sure what the problem in my thinking is, but I know there is one. Because I am lucky enough to have been an active partici-pant in forty years of both national and communal struggles for change, I know the richness of multiple visions. I call my writings offerings be-cause that is what they are: pieces of understanding or of questions, moments of intense pleasure or body-breaking pain–moments that you honor with your hearing. These offerings are as fragile as the body that lived them, my body, like yours.

Finally this is a book marked by leave-takings. The end of a ten-year relationship, a mundane pain in the world, but one that bent my words. The farewell to friends whose love and energy of purpose made my life glow. To my intimate daily contact with the Lesbian Herstory Archives, which after twenty years moved into its new home in a differ-ent borough, a home it desperately needed but whose absence I feel every day when I reach for the photograph or article or book that no longer greets me every morning and feel the emptiness of an apartment that no longer brims with the wonder of thousands of visitors bringing their pro-jects and dreams to my dining-room table. To my students, fragile in their youth but strong in their determination to forge new histories, who for twenty-nine years brought their words to me and who for a little while shared their cultural journeys with me in all their richness and complex-ity, in all their yearnings for safety and all their undertakings of risk.

But the wonder of life is change. My new publishers, Felice Newman and Frédérique Delacoste of Cleis Press, have given me the chance to write my own words again. Dianne Otto, a new friend and lover from Melbourne, Australia, has brought me a fuller understanding of love between women and an entryway into the world beyond my own country. I thank her for her attentive reading of my words and her willingness to take time from her own work to better inform mine. And to Lee Hudson, with whom I shared so much of the past, I look to the time when our strengths will reunite us.

I have experienced three sublimely beautiful things in my life, and each has been judged unacceptable by large parts of this society: the taste and touch of women lovers, the wondrous feeling of being part of a people working to free themselves, and for almost thirty years, the trust and attention of students many others did not want to teach. In my bed, in the streets of political protest, and in the classroom, I felt the possibilities of life most keenly, I saw the wonder of human hope and creativity most clearly. My students' heads bowed in concentration as they struggled to write for themselves and for me, my lover's head thrown back as she awaited the pressure of my tongue, my comrades' cold breath in the air as they stood their ground–these gifts, either so judged or dismissed, so problematical for some when put in the same sentence, cannot be isolated from one another. Made of fragile human dreams, but also of fierce desire, they have bound my life with joy.

New York
July 1998

I.
Letter to My Community

Letter to My Community:
A Sturdy Yes of a People

This public letter was written in 1993, after viewing the Senate hearings on gays in the military, after watching a Sixty Minutes *segment on the debate over the Rainbow Curriculum, and after months of reading debates over the humanity of gay people in the* New York Times.

These are not easy times, but they are times that must be. All around us, institutional heads debate our humanity as if we were not there, as if we were human objects to be moved around as their small minds and smaller hearts grapple with "the gay problem." Other people, working people, fierce in the protection of their children and in adherence to their religious leaders, pledge closed-mindedness. Devout Catholic, orthodox Jew, fundamental Christian know what God has said about us. The powerful and the powerless join hands in judgment.

But we come now a full-handed people. We come knowing our history, knowing our poets, knowing our communities from the past who built worlds for us to inherit. We come as women who refused to be ideal or childlike or fettered; we come as men who endured the loss of all for the love of some. We are the watchers of their sad shows; we can be the builders of new times.

For over four decades, I have made my way in this world as a lover of women. I have spread my legs and lowered my lips for the love of women at night and taught my students during the day. The way I loved filled the way I taught, the way I loved shaped the books I wrote, the way I loved shaped the politics of change I fought for. Hundreds of thousands of us held our passions close as we created public beauty in this country.

Offers will come to us: be silent, do not announce, tell no one and you will have a place. Silence wins no honest or safe place. Disclosures make us impossible; silence makes us possible. But our heritage demands sound–Radclyffe Hall shouts at her lawyer, "I mean this to be a book about inverts, not just friends." Oscar Wilde chides, "You cannot kill my love of young men by putting me in prison." Pat Parker asks in warning, "Where will you be when they come for you?" Mabel Hampton flaunts, "What do you mean, when did I come out? I was never *in*." Audre Lorde chants, "Silence will never save anyone." They cannot force silence into our mouths; we take lovers into our mouths, we take breasts and cock into our mouths, we take wetness and fullness into our mouths, but never their silence–for that will choke us.

Devout parents and family experts say we are inappropriate for children, that understanding is inappropriate for children, that meeting lesbian parents is harmful for children. Let them find out about these kinds of people when they are older, they say, as if we were a strange food for which only adults can have a taste. Let my child be beaten into manhood in the schoolyard, let my daughter lose her heart in the pursuit of a woman's life–but never let them know that gender is not a prison, that love is not always doled out to the same few. These people who wish to keep us from children battle to protect a killing ground.

Other excluded people have told us that perspective is all; Frederick Douglass wrote, "That which he most loved, I most hated, that which gave him life was death to me." The dying masters have built a house of cards, a full deck of hatreds, and are caught in its reflected images. We must know ourselves, know the solidity of our history and our gift of love, so we can walk through their mirrored house into the challenge waiting for us: the creation of a more just world.

Cohesion in the killing forces will be destroyed if we appear with our names full on our lips, say the military experts, all-powerful men sitting in the same chairs as the other men who judged what was real in other times–the House Un-American Activities Committee men, the Iran-Gate men, the Anita Hill men. Hollow voices they have become as we move forward, like ghosts they sit upon those chairs, mouthing the credos of a losing world; but even in their airy flailings, they maim hope.

Think of what they fear from us–love and desire, rebellion and difference, play, tenderness, touch, freer children who do not call each other faggot, girls who strive for their own glory, men who do not have to hate softness. All their words and reasons for exclusions, all the tumult of their No, will fall into the shadows of history.

You–my queer comrades–have given me a world where my words could live, where my love was kissed by sun, where my anger turned to visions of possibilities. These are hard times, but necessary ones. These are the times when we BE, a sturdy Yes of a people.

"I Lift My Eyes to the Hill": The Life of Mabel Hampton as Told by a White Woman

On Thursday nights, Mabel Hampton held court at the Lesbian Herstory Archives, opening the mail and gossiping with other archive workers. A devout collector of books on African American history and lesbian culture, in 1976 Ms. Hampton had donated her lesbian paperback collection to the archives. Surrounded by these books and many others, she shared in welcoming the visitors, some of whom had come just to meet her.

Another more public place we could count on finding Ms. Hampton in her later years was New York's Gay Pride march. From the early 1980s on, Ms. Hampton could be seen strutting down Fifth Avenue, *our* avenue for the day, marching under the Lesbian Herstory Archives banner, wearing her jauntily tilted black beret, her dark glasses, and a bright red T-shirt proclaiming her membership in SAGE (Senior Action in a Gay Environment). Later in the decade, when she could no longer walk the whole way, a crowd of younger lesbian women fought for the privilege to push her wheelchair down the avenue. Mabel Hampton, domestic worker, hospital matron, entertainer, had walked down many roads in her life–not always to cheering fans. Her persistent journey to full selfhood in a racist and capitalistic America is a story we are still learning to tell.

In recent years, I have been dazzled at our heady discussions of deconstruction, at our increasingly sophisticated academic conferences on gender representation, at the publication of sweeping communal and historical studies, and at our brave biographies of revered figures in American history in which the authors speak clearly about their subject's sexual identity. Mabel Hampton's is the story we are in danger of forgetting in our rush of language and queer theory.

Telling Mabel Hampton's history forces me to confront racism in my own relationship to her. Our two lives, Ms. Hampton's and mine, first intersected at a sadly traditional and suspect crossroads in the history of the relationships between black and white women in this country. These relationships are set in the mentality of a country that in the words of Professor Linda Meyers "could continue for over three hundred years to kidnap an estimated 50 million youths and young adults from Africa, transport them across the Atlantic with about half dying, unable to withstand the inhumanity of the passage."

In 1952, my small white Jewish mother took her breakfasts in a Bayside, Queens, luncheonette. Sitting next to her was a small black Christian woman. For several weeks they breakfasted together before they each went off to work, my mother to the office where she worked as a bookkeeper, Ms. Hampton to the homes she cleaned and the children she cared for.

One morning, Ms. Hampton told me, she followed my mother out to her bus to say good-bye and my mother, Regina, threw the keys to our apartment out the bus window, asking whether Ms. Hampton would consider working for her. "I told her I would give her a week's trial," Ms. Hampton said.

This working relationship was not to last long because of my mother's own financial instability, but the friendship between my mother and Ms. Hampton did. I remember Ms. Hampton caring for me when I was ill. I remember her tan raincoat with a lesbian paperback in its pocket, its jacket bent back so no one could see the two women in the shadows on its cover. I remember, when I was twelve years old, asking my mother as we did laundry together one weekend whose men's underwear we were washing since no man lived in our apartment. "They are Mabel's," she said.

In future years, Regina, Mabel, and Mabel's wife Lillian became closer friends, bound together by a struggle to survive and by my mother's lesbian daughter. Ms. Hampton told me during one of our afternoons together that when Regina suspected I was a lesbian she called her late one night and threatened to kill herself if I turned out that way. "I told her, she might as well go ahead and do it because it wasn't her business what her daughter did and besides, I'm one and it suits me fine."

Because Ms. Hampton and I later formed an adult relationship, based on our commitment to a lesbian community, I had a chance much later in life, when Ms. Hampton herself needed care, to reverse the image this society thrives on, that of black women caring for white people. The incredulous responses we both received in my Upper West Side apartment building when I was Ms. Hampton's caretaker showed how deeply the traditional racial script still resonated. To honor her, to touch her again, to be honest in the face of race, to refuse the blankness of physical death, to share the story of her own narrative of liberation–for all these reasons–it is she I must write about.

Ms. Hampton pointed the way her story should be told. Her legacy of documents so carefully assembled for Deborah Edel, who had met Ms. Hampton in the early seventies and who had all of Ms. Hampton's trust, tell in no uncertain terms that her life revolved around two major themes–her material struggle to survive and her cultural struggle for beauty. Bread and roses, the worker's old anthem–this is what I want to remember, the texture of the individual life of a working woman.

After her death on October 26, 1989, when Deborah and I were gathering her papers, we found a box carefully marked, "In case I pass away see that Joan and Deb get this at once, Mabel." On top of the pile of birth certificates and cemetery plot contracts was a piece of lined paper with the following typed entries:

> 1915–1919: 8B, Public School 32, Jersey City
> 1919–1923: Housework, Dr. Kraus, Jersey City
> 1923–1927: Housework, Mrs. Parker, Jersey City
> 1927–1931: Housework, Mrs. Katim, Brooklyn
> 1932–1933: Housework, Dr. Garland, New York City
> 1934–1940: Daily housework, different homes
> 1941–1944: Matron, Hammarlund Manufacturing Co., NYC
> 1945–1953: Housework, Mrs. Jean Nate
> 1948–1955: Attendant, New York Hospital
> 1954–1955: General, daily work
> Lived 1935: 271 West 122nd Street, NYC
> Lived 1939–1945: West 111th Street, NYC
> Lived 1945–current (1955): 663 East 169th Street, Bronx, NYC

Compiled in the mid-fifties when Ms. Hampton was applying for a position at Jacobi Hospital, the list demanded attention–a list so bare and yet so eloquent of a life of work and home.

Since 1973, the start of the Lesbian Herstory Archives, I have felt Ms. Hampton's story must be told, but I am not a trained historian or sociologist. However, in the seventies, training workshops in doing oral histories with gay people were popping up around the city, and I attended every session I could. There, Jonathan Katz, Liz Kennedy, Madeline Davis, and I would talk for hours, trying to come up with the questions that we thought would elicit the kind of history we wanted: What did you call yourself in the twenties? How did you and your friends dress in the forties? What bars did you go to? In the late seventies, when I started doing oral history tapes with Ms. Hampton, I quickly learned how limited our methods were.

J.: Do you remember anything about sports? Did you know women who liked to play softball? Were there any teams?

M.: No, all the women, they didn't care too much about them—softballs—they liked the soft women. Didn't care about any old softball. Cut it out!

I soon realized that Ms. Hampton had her own narrative style, which was tightly connected to how she had made sense of her life, but it wasn't until I had gone through every piece of paper she had bequeathed us that I had a deeper understanding of what her lesbian life had meant.

Lesbian and gay scholars argue over whether we can call a woman a lesbian who lived in a time when that word was not used. We have been very careful about analyzing how our social sexual representation was created by medical terminology and cultural terrors. But here was a different story. Ms. Hampton's lesbian history is embedded in the history of race and class in this country; she makes us extend our historical perspective until she is at its center. The focus then is not lesbian history but lesbians *in* history.

When asked "Ms. Hampton, when did you come out?" she loved to flaunt, "What do you mean? I was never *in!*" Her audiences always cheered this assertion of lesbian identity, but now I think Ms. Hampton was speaking of something more inclusive.

Driven to fend for herself as an orphan, as a black working woman, as a lesbian, Ms. Hampton always struggled to fully occupy her life, refusing to be cut off from the communal, national, and worldly events around her. She was never in, in any aspect of her life, if being "in" means withholding the fullest response possible from what life is demanding of you at the moment.

Along her way, Ms. Hampton found and created communities for comfort and support, communities that engendered her fierce loyalty. Her street in the Bronx, 169th Street, was *her* street, and she walked it as "Miss Mabel," known to all and knowing all, whether it was the woman representing her congressional district or the numbers runner down the block. How she occupied this street, this moment in urban twentieth-century American history, is very similar to how she occupied her life–self-contained but always visible, carrying her own sense of how life should be lived but generous to those who were struggling to make a decent life out of indecent conditions.

I cannot re-create the whole of Ms. Hampton's life, but I can follow her journey up to the 1950s by blending the documents she left, such as letters, newspaper clippings, and programs, with excerpts from her oral history and my interpretations and readings of other sources.

These personal daily documents represent the heart of the Lesbian Herstory Archives; they are the fragile records of a tough woman who never took her eyes off the hilltop, who never let racism destroy her love for her own culture, who never let the tyranny of class keep her from finding the beauty she needed to live, who never accepted her traditional woman's destiny, and who never let hatred and fear of lesbians keep her from her gay community.

None of it was easy. From the beginning, Ms. Hampton had to run for her life.

Desperate to be considered for employment by the City of New York, Ms. Hampton began to document her own beginnings in April of 1963:

To the county clerk in the Hall of Records, Winston-Salem, North Carolina: "Gentlemen: I would appreciate very much your helping me to secure my birth papers or any record you may have on file, as to my birth and proof of age as this information is vital for the purpose of my securing a civil service position in New York. Listed below are the information I have to help you locate any records you may have.

"I was born approximately May 2, 1902 in Winston-Salem. My mother's name was Lulu Hampton or Simmons. I attended Teacher's College which is its name now at the age of six. My grandmother's name was Simmons. I lived there with her after the death of my mother when I was two months old. It is very important to me as it means a livelihood for me to secure any information."

On an affidavit of birth dated May 26, 1943, we find this additional information: Ms. Hampton was of the Negro race, her father's full name was Joseph Hampton (a fact she did not discover until she was almost twenty years old), and he had been born in Reidsville, North Carolina. Her mother's birthplace was listed as Lynchburg, Virginia.

This appeal for a record of her beginnings points us to where Ms. Hampton's history began; not in the streets of Greenwich Village, where she will sing for pennies thrown from windows in 1910 at the age of eight, not even in Winston-Salem, where she will live on her grandmother's small farm from her birth until 1909, but further back into a past of a people, further back into the shame of a country.

Ms. Hampton's deepest history lies in the middle passage of the Triangular Slave Trade, and before that in the complex and full world of sixteenth-century Africa. When Europe turned its ambitious face to the curving coastline of the ancient continent and created an economic system based on the servitude of Africans, Ms. Hampton's story began. The middle passage, the horrendous crossing of the waters from Africa to this side of the world, literally and figuratively became the time of generational loss. Millions died in those waters, carrying their histories with them. This tragic "riddle in the waters," as the Afro-Cuban poet Nicolás Guillén calls it, was continued on the land of the southern plantation system. Frederick Douglass writes, "I have no accurate knowledge of my age, never having seen any authentic record containing it." These words were written in 1845 and Ms. Hampton was born in 1902, but now as I reflect on Ms. Hampton's dedication to preserving her own documents, I read them as a moment in the history of an African American lesbian.

The two themes of work and communal survival that run so strongly throughout Ms. Hampton's life are prefigured by the history of black working women in the sharecropping system, a history told in great moving detail by Jacqueline Jones in her study, *Labor of Love, Labor of Sorrow: Black Women, Work, and Family from Slavery to the Present*. Though Ms. Jones never mentions lesbian women, Ms. Hampton and her wife of forty-five years, Lillian Foster, who was born in Norfolk, Virginia, carried on in their lesbian lives traditions that had their roots in the post-slavery support systems created by southern black women at the turn of the century. The comradeship of these all-women benevolent and mutual aid societies was rediscovered by Ms. Hampton and Ms. Foster in their New York chapters of the Eastern Star.

Even the work both the women did, domestic service for Ms. Hampton and pressing for Ms. Foster, had its roots in this earlier period. Jones tells us that "in the largest southern cities from 50 to 70 percent of all black women were gainfully employed at least part of the year around the turn of the century." In Durham, North Carolina, close to Ms. Hampton's birthplace, during the period of 1880–1910, "one hundred percent of all black female household heads, aged 20 to 24, were wage earners." Very likely, both Ms. Hampton's grandmother and her mother were part of this workforce.

"I'm Mabel Hampton. I was born on May the second 1902, in Winston-Salem, North Carolina, and I left there when I was eight years old. Grandma said I was so small that [my] head was as big as a silver dollar. She said that she did all she could to make me grow. One day she was making the bed and gettin' things together after she fed the chickens. She never let me lay in the bed; I lay in the rocking chair, and this day she put the clothes in the chair; when she carried 'em outside, she forgot I was in 'em and shook the clothes out and shook me out in the garden out on the ground. And Grandma was so upset that she hurt me.

"My grandmother took care of me. My mother died two months after I was born. She was poisoned, which left me with just my grandma, mother's younger sister, and myself. We had a house and lived on a street—we had chickens, had hogs, garden vegetables, grapes and things. We had a backyard, I can see it right now, that backyard. It had red roses, white roses, roses that went upside the house. We never had to go to the store for anything. On Saturdays we go out hunting blackberries, strawberries, and peaches. My girlfriends lived on each side of the street: Anna Lou Thomas, Hattie Harris, Lucille Crump. Oh-OOh-O Anna Lou Thomas, she was good lookin', she was a good-lookin' girl.

"One day Grandma says, 'Mabel I'm goin' to take you away.' She left Sister there and we went to Lynchburg, Virginia, because Grandma's mother had died. I remember when I got there, the man picked me up off the floor and I looked down on this woman who had drifts of gray hair. She was kind of a brown-skinned woman and she was good lookin'. Beautiful gray hair she had. I looked at her and then he put me down on a stool and I set there. They sang and prayed and carried on. I went to sleep."

However pleasant Ms. Hampton's memories were of North Carolina, she had no intention of returning there later in her life. "Lillian tried her best to get me to go to Winston-Salem. I says, 'No, I don't want to.' She says, 'You wouldn't even go to my home?' I says 'No, because with my nasty temper they'd lynch me in five minutes. Because they would see me walkin' down the street holdin' hands with some woman, they want to put me in jail. Now I can hold hands with some woman all over New York, all over the Bronx and everywhere else and no one says nothing to me.' "

When she was seven years old, in 1909, Ms. Hampton was forced to migrate to New York. In her own telling there is a momentous sense that she lost whatever safety she had in that garden of roses.

"One morning I was in the bedroom getting ready for school [*a deep sigh*]. I heard Grandma go out in the yard and come back and then I heard a big bump on the floor. So I ran to the door and I looked and Grandma was laying stretched out on the floor. I hollered and hollered and they all came running and picked her up and put her on the bed. She had had a stroke. Grandma lived one week after she had that stroke. My mama's younger aunt, I'll never forget it, was combing my hair and I looked over at Grandma layin' in bed. It was in the morning. The sun was up and everything. She looked at me and I looked at her. And when my aunt got finished combing my hair, Grandma had gone away.

"They called my mother's sister in New York and she came so fast I think she was there the next day. I remember the day we left Winston-Salem. It was in the summertime. We went by train and I had a sandwich of liver between two pieces of bread. And I knew and felt then that things was going to be different. After eating that sandwich I cried all the way to New York. My aunt tried to pacify me but it didn't do no good, seems as if my heart was broken."

Taken to a small apartment at 52 West Eighth Street, Ms. Hampton meets her uncle, a minister, who, within the year, will rape her.

In telling her story Ms. Hampton has given two reasons for her running away at age eight from this home: one involves a fight with a white girl at school and the other, a terrible beating by her uncle after she had misspelled a word. Whatever the exact reason, it was clear that Ms. Hampton had already decided she needed another air to breathe.

"My aunt went out one day and he raped me. I said to myself, 'I've got to leave here.' He wouldn't let me sleep in the bed. They had a place where they put coal at, and he put a blanket down and made me lay there. So this day, I got tired of that. I went out with nothing on but a dress, a jumper dress, and I walked and walked."

Here begins an amazing tale of an eight-year-old girl's odyssey to find a place and a way to live. After walking the streets for hours, the young Ms. Hampton "comes to a thing in the ground, in the sidewalk, people was going down there." A woman comes by and thinks she recognizes the lost child. "Aren't you Miss Brown's little girl?" Before Ms. Hampton can answer, she places a nickel in her hand and tells her to go back home to Harlem. As Ms. Hampton says, "that nickel was a turning point in my life."

Instead of going uptown, Ms. Hampton boarded a Jersey-bound train and rode to the last stop. She came above ground and walked until she found a playground. "I seen all these children playin', white and black, all of them havin' a good time." She joins the children and plays until it begins to get dark. Two of the children take an interest in her and she makes up a story: "My aunt told me to stay here until she comes." The girl calls to her brother, "You go get the cops, I'll try to find her aunt." She brings a woman back with her–a Miss Bessie White–who begins to ask her questions. Ms. Hampton: "I looked down the street and from the distance I see the boy comin' with the cop so I decided to go with the woman. Bessie said, 'Come, I'll take you home.'"

Ms. Hampton will remain with the White family until she is seventeen years old. One member of the family, Ellen, particularly stays in her memory: "I seen a young woman sitting left of where I come in at. I say to myself, this is a good-looking woman; I was always admiring some woman. Oh, and she was. She had beautiful hair and she looked just like an angel. She got up out of the chair, she was kind of tall, and she says 'you come with me.' So she took me upstairs, bathed me, and said 'we'll find you some clothes.' She always talked very softly. And she says, 'you'll sleep with me.' I was glad of that.

"So I went and stayed with them. The other sister went on about lookin' for my aunt. I knew she never find her. See, I knew everything about me, but I kept quiet. I kept quiet for twenty years."

Mabel Hampton, from the very beginning of her narrative, speaks with the determination of a woman who must take care of herself. She will decide what silences to keep and what stories to tell, creating for herself a power over life's circumstances that her material resources seldom gave her.

For Mabel Hampton, the 1920s were both a decade of freedom and one of literal imprisonment. In 1919, when she is seventeen years old, she is doing housework for a Dr. Kraus of Jersey City. Her beloved Ellen, the first woman friend to hold Ms. Hampton in her arms, has died during childbirth. With Ellen gone, Ms. Hampton's ties to the White family are loosening; she will find work dancing in an all-women's company that performs in Coney Island and have her first requited lesbian love affair. She will discover the club life of New York. This is the decade in which Ms. Hampton will pay a visit to the salon of A'Lelia Walker, the flapper daughter of Madam Walker, and be amazed at the multiple sexual couplings she observes. She will perform in the Lafayette Theater and dance at the Garden of Joy, both in Harlem. In this decade, she will make the acquaintance of Ethel Waters, Gladys Bentley, and Alberta Hunter. She will be one of the 150,000 mourners who sing "My Buddy" as the casket bearing Florence Mills, beloved singer, slowly moves through the Harlem streets in 1927. This is Ms. Hampton's experience of the period that lives in history books as the Harlem Renaissance.

But before all this exploration takes place, Ms. Hampton will be arrested for prostitution by two white policemen and be sentenced to three years in Bedford Hills Reformatory for Women by a Judge Norris. Ms. Hampton: "While we're standing there talking, the door opens. Now I know I had shut it. And two white men walk in–great big white men. 'We're raiding this house,' one of them says. 'For what?' 'Prostitution,' he says. I hadn't been with a man no time. I couldn't figure it out. I didn't have time to get clothes or nothing. The judge she sat up there and says 'Well, only thing I can say is Bedford.' No lawyer, no nothing. She railroaded me."

When Ms. Hampton talks about her prison experience, she dwells on the kindnesses she found there: "It was summertime and we went back out there and sat down. She [another prisoner] says 'I like you.' 'I like you too.' She said no more until time to go to bed. We went to bed and she took me in her bed and held me in her arms and I went to sleep. She put her arms around me like Ellen used to do, you know, and I went to sleep."

But where Ms. Hampton found friendship, the board of managers of the prison found scandal and disgrace. Opened in 1902 in a progressive era of prison reform, Bedford Hills under its first woman administrator, Katherine Davis, accepted the special friendships of its women inmates. But in 1920, word that interracial lesbian sex was occurring throughout the prison caused Ms. Davis to lose her job. The new administrators of the prison demanded segregated facilities, the only way, according to one of the men, to prevent interracial sex.

By the time I was doing the oral history with Ms. Hampton, she had left this experience far behind. She told me that she seldom told anyone about it; she would just say she had gone away for a while. But toward the end of her life, Ms. Hampton wanted her whole story to be told. She realized that her desire to be open about her life was not popular with her peers. "So many of my friends got religion now," she would say, "you can't get anything out of them."

While Mabel Hampton so generously shared her prison experience with me, I read about Bedford Hills in Estelle Freedman's book, *Their Sister's Keepers: Women's Prison Reform in America, 1830-1930*. When I read the following sentence in Freedman's book, "By 1919, we are told, about 75% of the prisoners were prostitutes, 70% had venereal disease, a majority were of low mental ability and ten percent were psychopaths," I was forced to see the lesbians encoded in this list. Mabel Hampton was among these counted women. As gays and lesbians, we have a special insight, a special charge in doing history work. We, too, have had our humanity hidden in such lists of undesirables. I started this work on Mabel Hampton because her life brought to the study of history the dignity of the human face behind the sweeping summaries. And because I loved her.

After thirteen months, Ms. Hampton is released from prison

with the condition that she stay away from New York City and its bad influences. But Ms. Hampton cannot contain herself. A white woman with a gray car whom she met in Bedford comes to Jersey City to take her to parties in New York. When a neighbor informs on her, she is forced to return and complete her sentence at Bedford. Ms. Hampton later describes some of the life that the state had declared criminal.

"In 1923, I am about twenty years old. I had rooms at 120 West 122nd street. A girlfriend of mine was living next door and they got me three rooms there on the ground floor—a bedroom, living room, and big kitchen. I stayed there until I met Lillian in 1932. I went away with the people I worked for, but I always kept my rooms to come back to. Then I went into the show.

"Next door these girls were all lesbians, they had four rooms in the basement and they gave parties all the time. Sometimes we would have 'pay parties.' We'd buy all the food—chicken and potato salads. I'd chip in with them because I would bring my girlfriends. We also went to 'rent parties' where you go in and pay a couple of dollars. You buy your drinks and meet other women and dance and have fun. But with our house we just had close friends. Sometimes there would be twelve or fourteen women there. We'd have pig feet, chittlins. In the wintertime, it was black-eyed peas and all that stuff. Most of the women wore suits. Very seldom did any of them have slacks or anything like that, because they had to come through the streets. Of course, if they were in a car, they wore the slacks. Most of them had short hair. And most of them was good-lookin' women too. The bulldykers would come and bring their women with them. And you wasn't supposed to jive with them, you know. They danced up a breeze. They did the Charleston, they did a little bit of every-thing. They were all colored women. Sometimes we ran into someone who had a white woman with them. But me, I'd venture out with any of them. I just had a ball.

"I had a couple of white girlfriends down in the village. We got along fine. At that time I was acting in the Cherry Lane Theater. I didn't have to go to the bars because I would go to women's houses. Like Jackie (Moms) Mabley would have a big party and all the girls from the show would go. She had all the women there."

In addition to private parties, Ms. Hampton and her friends were up on the latest public lesbian events. Sometime in February of 1927, Ms. Hampton attended the new play that was scandalizing Broadway, *The Captive*. Whatever her material struggle was in any given decade, Ms. Hampton sought out the cultural images she needed. Here, in a brief excerpt, is how she remembered that night at the theater.

Well, I heard about it and a girlfriend of mine had taken me to see this play, *The Captive*. and I fell in love–not only with *The Captive*, but the lady who was the head actress in it. Her name was Helen Mencken. So I decided I would go back–I had heard so much talk about it. I went back to see it by myself. I sat on the edge of my seat! I looked at the first part and I will always think that woman was a lesbian. She played it too perfect! She had the thing down! She kissed too perfect, she had everything down pat. So that's why I kept going back to see it, because it looked like to me it was part of my life. I was a young woman, but I said now this is what I would like to be, but of course, I would have to marry and I didn't want to marry [the play focuses on the seduction of a married woman by the offstage lesbian, who is also married], so I would just go on and do whatever I thought was right to do. I talked to a couple of my friends in Jersey City about the play. I carried them back, paid their way to see it, and they fell in love with it. There was plenty of women in that audience and plenty of men too! They applauded and applauded. This same girl with the green car, she knew her–Helen Mencken–and she carried me backstage and introduced me. Boy, I felt so proud! And she says, "Why do you like the show?" I said, "Because it seems a part of my life and what I am and what I hope to be." She says, "That's nice. Stick to it! You'll be alright."

The 1920s end with Mabel Hampton living fully "in the life," trying to piece together another kind of living from her day work and from her chorus line jobs. Later, when asked why she left show business, she will say, "Because I like to eat."

The Depression does not play a large role in Ms. Hampton's memories, perhaps because she was already earning such a marginal income. We know that from 1925 until 1937, she did day work for the family of Charles Baubrick. Ms. Hampton carefully saved all the letters from her employees testifying to her character:

"Dec. 12, 1937: To Whom It May Concern: This is to certify that the bearer Mabel Hampton has worked for me for the last 12 years doing housework off and on and she does the same as yet. We have always found her honest and industrious."

Reading these letters, embedded as they were in all the other documents of Ms. Hampton's life, is always sobering. So much of her preserved papers testify to an autonomous home and social life, but these formal letters sprinkled through each decade remind us that in some sense Ms. Hampton's life was under surveillance by the white families who controlled her economic survival.

In 1935, Ms. Hampton is baptized into the Roman Catholic Church at St. Thomas the Apostle on West 118th Street, another step in her quest for spiritual comfort. This journey would include a lifelong devotion to the mysteries of the Rosicrucians and a full collection of Marie Corelli, a Victorian novelist with a spiritualist bent. She will end the decade registering with the United States Department of Labor trying to find a job. She is told, "We will get in touch with you as soon as there is a suitable opening."

The event that changes Ms. Hampton's life forever happens early on in the decade, in 1932: while waiting for a bus, she meets a woman even smaller than herself, "dressed like a duchess," as Ms. Hampton would later say: Lillian Foster.

Ms. Foster remembers in 1976, two years before her death:

"Forty-four years ago I met Mabel. We was a wonderful pair. I'll never regret it. But she's a little tough. I met her in 1932, September twenty-second. And we haven't been separated since in our whole life. Death will separate us. Other than that I don't want it to end."

Ms. Hampton, to the consternation of her more discreet friends, dressed in an obvious way much of her life. Her appearance, however, did not seem to bother her wife. Ms. Foster goes on to say: "A lady walked in once, Joe's wife, and she say, 'You is a pretty neat girl. You have a beautiful little home but where is your husband?' And just at that time, Mabel comes in the door with her key and I said, 'There is my husband.' " The visitor added, "Now you know if that was your husband, you wouldn't have said it!" to which Ms. Foster firmly replied, "But I said it!"

Lillian Foster, born in 1906 in Norfolk, Virginia, shared much of the same southern background of Ms. Hampton, except that she came from a large family. She was keenly aware that Ms. Hampton was "all alone," as she often put it. Ms. Foster worked her whole life as a presser in white-owned dry-cleaning establishments, a job, like domestic service, that had its roots in the neo-slavery working conditions of the urban South at the turn of the century. These many years of labor in underventilated back rooms accelerated Ms. Foster's rapid decline in her later years. But together with a group of friends, these two women would create a household lasting for forty-six years.

This household with friends took many shapes. When crisis struck and a fire destroyed their apartment in 1976, as part of the real estate wars that were gutting and leveling the Bronx, Ms. Foster and Ms. Hampton came to live with me and Deborah Edel until they could move back to their home. Later, Ms. Hampton would describe our shared time as an adventure in lesbian families. "Down here it was just like two couples, Joan and Deborah and Mabel and Lillian; we got along lovely, and we played, we sang, we ate; it was marvelous! I will never forget it. And Lillian, of course, Lillian was my wife. I had Joan laughing because I called Lillian 'Little Bear,' but when I first met her in 1932, she was to me, she was a duchess–the grand duchess. Later in life I got angry with her one day and I called her the 'little bear' and she called me 'the big bear' and of course that hung on to me all through life. And now we are known to all our friends as the 'big bear' and the 'little bear.'

Ms. Hampton saved hundreds of cards signed 'Little bear.' But when she appealed to government officials or agencies for help, as she often did as their housing conditions deteriorated, she said Ms. Foster was her sister.

Letter to Mayor Lindsay, 1969:

"Dear Mr. Mayor, I don't know if I am on the right road or not, but I am taking a chance; now what I want to know is can you tell me how I can get an apartment, I have been everywhere and no success. I am living at the above address [639 E. 169th Street, Bronx] for 26 years but for about the past 10 years the building has gone down terribly. For two years we have no heat all winter, also no hot water. We called the housing authority but it seems it don't help; everywhere I go the rent is so high that poor people can't pay it and I would like to find a place before the winter comes in with rent that I can afford to pay. It is two of us (women) past 65. I still work but my older sister is on retirement so we do need two bedrooms. If you can do something to help us it will be greatly appreciated.

Thanking you in advance,
I remain, Miss Mabel Hampton.

Finding this letter marked a turning point in my work. Ms. Hampton's request for a safe and warm home for herself and Ms. Foster now stands as the starting point of all my historical inquiry: How did you survive?

In a document of a different sort, the program for a social event sponsored by Jacobi hospital, where she was employed for the last twenty years of her working life, we discover that a Ms. Mabel Hampton and Ms. Lillian Hampton are sitting at Table 25. These two women negotiated the public world as "sisters," which allowed expressions of affection and demanded a recognition of their intimacy.

There is a seamless quality to Ms. Hampton's life that does not fit our usual paradigm for doing lesbian history work. Her life does not seem to be organized around what we have come to see as the usual rites of gay passage, like coming out or going to the bars. Instead, she gives us the vision of an integrated life in which the major shaping events are the daily acts of work, friends, and social organizations, and the major definers of these territories are class and race; in addition, she expects all aspects of her life to be respected.

Every letter preserved by Ms. Hampton written by a friend, co-worker, or employer contains a greeting or a blessing for Ms. Foster. "I do hope to be able to visit you and Lillian some evening for a real chat and a supper by a superb cook! Do take care of yourself and my best to Lillian," Dolores, 1944; "God bless and keep you and Lillian well always, I wish I could see you both some times," Jennie, 1977.

The 1940s were turbulent years, marked by World War II and unrest at home. While African American soldiers were fighting the armies of racial supremacists in Europe, their families were fighting the racist dictates of a Jim Crow society at home. Harlem, Detroit, and other American cities would see streets become battlefields.

For African American working women like Ms. Hampton, the 1940s was the decade of the slave markets, the daily gathering of Black women on the street corners of Brooklyn and the Bronx to sell their domestic services to white women who drove by looking for cheap labor. In 1940, Ms. Hampton was part of this labor force as she had been for over twenty years, working year after year without worker's compensation, health benefits, or pension payments.

In September of 1940, she receives a postcard canceling her employment with one family: "Dear Mabel, please do not come on Thursday. I will see you again on Friday at Mrs. Garfinkels. I have engaged a part time worker as I need more frequent help as you know. Come over to see us."

Ms. Hampton did not let her working difficulties dampen her enthusiasm for her cultural heroes, however. On October 6, 1940, she and Ms. Foster are in the audience at Carnegie Hall, when at 8:30 P.M., Paul Robeson commands the stage. The announcement for this concert is the first document we have reflecting Ms. Hampton's lifelong love of the opera and her dedication to African American cultural figures and institutions.

In 1941, perhaps in recognition of her perilous situation as a day worker, Ms. Hampton secures the job of matron with the Hammarlund Manufacturing Company on West Thirty-Fourth Street, assuring her entrance into the new social security system begun just six years earlier by Franklin Roosevelt.

She still takes irregular night and day domestic employment so she and Ms. Foster can, among other things, on May 28, 1946, purchase from the American Mending Machine Company one Singer Electric Sewing Machine with console table for the price of $100. She leaves a $44 deposit and carefully preserves all records of the transaction.

On February 20, 1942, we have the first evidence of Ms. Hampton's involvement in the country's war efforts: a ditto sheet of instructions from the American Women's Voluntary Services addressed to all air raid wardens. "During the German attack on the countries of Europe, the telephone was often used for sabotage thereby causing panic and loss of life by erroneous orders. We in New York are particularly vulnerable in this respect since our great apartment houses have often hundreds even thousands under one roof.... The apartment house telephone warden must keep lines clear in time of emergency. Type of person required: this sort of work should be particularly suited for women whose common sense and reliability could be depended upon."

In August, Ms. Hampton is working hard for the Harlem branch of the New York Defense Recreation Committee, trying to collect cigarettes and other refreshments for the soldiers and sailors who frequent

Harlem's USO. In December of 1942, she is appointed deputy sector commander in the air warden service by Mayor LaGuardia. This same year she will also receive her American Theater Wing War Service membership card. Throughout 1943, she serves as her community's air raid warden and attends monthly meetings of the 12th Division of the American Women's Voluntary Services Organizations on West 116th Street. During all this time, her country will maintain a segregated army abroad and a segregated society at home.

In January and February of 1944, she receives her fourth and fifth war loan citation. This support for causes she believed in, no matter how small her income, continues throughout Ms. Hampton's life. In addition to her religious causes, for example, she will send monthly donations to SCLC and the Martin Luther King Memorial Fund; by the end of the seventies, she is adding gay organizations to her list.

On March 29, 1944, Ms. Hampton attends the National Negro Opera Company's performance of *La Traviata*. This group believed in opera for the masses and included in its program a congratulatory message from the Upper West Side Communist Party. On its board sat Eleanor Roosevelt and Mary McCloud Bethune, both part of another moment in lesbian history. In 1952, this same company will present *Ouanga*, an opera based on the life of the first king of Haiti, Dessaline, who the program says "successfully conquered Napoleon's armies in 1802 and won the Black Republic's fight for freedom." Ms. Hampton will be in the audience.

Continuing her dedication to finding the roses amid the struggle, on November 12, 1944, Ms. Hampton will hear Marian Anderson sing at Carnegie Hall and add the program of this event to her collection of newspaper articles about the career of this valiant woman.

Ms. Hampton's never-ending pursuit of work often caused long absences from home, and Ms. Foster was often left waiting for her partner to return to their Bronx apartment on 169th Street, the apartment they had moved into in 1945, at the war's end, and which would remain their shared home until Ms. Foster's death in 1978.

Dear Mabel:

Received your letter and was very glad to hear from you and to know that you are well and happy. This leaves me feeling better than I have since you left. Everything is OK at home. Only I miss you so much I will be glad when the time is up. There is nobody like you to me. I am writing this on my lunch hour. It is 11 P.M. I am quitting tomorrow. I don't see anyone as I haven't been feeling too well. Well the ½ hour is up. Nite nite be good and will see you soon.

Little Bear

In 1948, Ms. Hampton falls ill and cannot work. She applies for home relief and is awarded a grant of $54.95 a month, which the agency stipulates should be spent the following way: $27 for food; $21 for rent; 55¢ for cooking fuel; 80¢ for electricity; $6 for clothing, and for personal incidentals, she is allotted $1. But from these meager funds she manages to give comfort to friends.

Postcard, August 9, 1948:

Dear Miss Lillian and Mabel:

The flowers you sent were beautiful and I liked them very much. I wear the heart you sent all the time. It was very nice to hear from you both. I am feeling fine now. I hope you are both in the best of health.

Love
Doris

In 1949, Ms. Hampton writes to the home relief agency telling the caseworker to stop all payments because she has the promise of a job.

The decade that began in war between nations and peoples ends in Ms. Hampton's version of history with a carefully preserved article about the international figure Josephine Baker. Cut out of the March 12, 1949, issue of *The Pittsburgh Courier* are the following words:

Well friends, fellow Negroes and countrymen, you can stop all that guesswork and surmising about Josephine Baker. This writer knew Edith Spencer, Lottie Gee, Florence Mills, knew them well. He has also known most of the other colored women artists of the last thirty years. His word to you is that this Josephine Baker eminently belongs. She is not a common music hall entertainer. She has been over here for a long time, maybe 25 years. The little old colored gal from back home is a French lady now. That means something. It means for a colored person that you have been accepted into a new and glamorous and free world where color does not count. It means that in the joy of the new living you just might forget that "old oaken bucket" so full of bitter quaffs for you. It means that once you found solid footing in the new land of freedom, you might tax your mind to blot out all the sorry past, all the old associations, to become alien in spirit as well as in fact. It pleases me folks to be able to report to you that none of this has possessed Josephine. I tested her and she rang true. What she does is for you and me. She said so out of her own mouth. Her eyes glistened as she expostulated and described in vivid, charged phrases the aim and purpose of her work. She was proud when I told her of Lena and of Hilda [Simms]. "You girls are blazing trails for the race," I commentated. "Indeed so," she quickly retorted. After she had talked at length of what it means to be a Negro and of her hope that whatever she did might reflect credit on Negroes, particularly the Negroes of her land of birth, I chanced a leading question. "So you're a race woman," I queried. I was not sure she would understand. But she did. "Of course I am," she replied. Yes, all the world's a stage and Josephine comes out upon it for you and for me.

In my own work, I have tried to focus on the complex interaction between oppression and resistance, aware of the dangers of romanticizing losses while at the same time aggrandizing little victories, but I am still awed by how a single human spirit refuses the messages of self-hatred and out of bits and pieces weaves a garment grand enough for the soul's and body's passion. Ms. Hampton prized her memories of Josephine Baker, Marian Anderson, and Paul Robeson, creating for herself a nurturing family of defiant African American women and men. Her lesbian self was part of what was fed by their soaring voices. When the *New York Times* closed its obituary on Ms. Hampton with the words "There are no known survivors," it showed its ignorance of how an oppressed people make legacies out of memory.

In our history of Ms. Hampton, we are now entering the so-called conforming 1950s, when white, middle-class heterosexual women, we have been told, are running in droves to be married and keep the perfect home. Reflecting another vision, Ms. Hampton carefully cuts out and saves newspaper articles on the pioneer transsexual Christine Jorgensen. From 1948 until her retirement in 1972, Ms. Hampton will work in the housekeeping division of Jacobi Hospital, where she earns for herself the nickname "Captain" from some of the women she works with, who keep in touch with Ms. Hampton until their deaths many years later. Here she meets Ms. Jorgensen and pays her nightly visits in her hospital room.

From Ms. Hampton's documents: *Daily News* article, December 1, 1952, "Ex-GI Becomes Blond Beauty," contains a letter written by Jorgensen explaining to her parents why there is so much consternation about her case. She concludes, "It is more a problem of social taboos and the desire not to speak of the subject because it deals with the great hush hush, namely sex."

Ms. Hampton begins the decade earning $1,006 for a year's work and ends it earning $1,232. Because of lack of money, Ms. Hampton was never able to travel to all the places in the world that fascinated her; but in this decade she adds hundreds of pages of stamps to her overflowing albums, little squares of color from Morroco and Zanzibar, from the Philippines and Mexico.

Throughout her remaining years, Ms. Hampton will continue with her eyes on the hilltop and her feet on a very earthly pavement. She will always have very little money and will always be generous. In the

1970s, Ms. Hampton discovers senior citizen centers and "has a ball," as she liked to say, on their subsidized trips to Atlantic City. She will lose her partner of forty-five years, Lillian Foster, in 1978.

After almost drifting away in mourning, she will find new energy and a loving family in New York's lesbian and gay community. She will have friendly visitors from SAGE and devoted friends like Ann Allen Shockley, who never fails to visit when she is in town. She will march in Washington in the first national lesbian and gay civil rights march. She will appear in films like *Silent Pioneers* and *Before Stonewall.* In 1987, she accompanies Deborah and her lover Teddy to California so she can be honored at the West Coast Old Lesbians Conference.

She will eventually have to give up her fourth-floor walk-up Bronx apartment and move in with Lee Hudson and myself, who along with many others will care for her as she loses physical strength. On October 26, 1989, after a second stroke, Ms. Hampton will finally let go of a life she loved so dearly.

Ms. Hampton never relented in her struggle to live a fully integrated life, a life marked by the integrity of her self-authorship. "If I give you my word," she always said, "I'll be there"–and she was.

On her death, her sisters in Electa Chapter 10 of the Eastern Star Organization honored her with the following words: "We wish to express our gratitude for having known Sister Hampton all these years. She became a member many years ago and went from the bottom to the top of the ladder. She has served us in many capacities. We loved her dearly. May she rest in peace with the angels."

Class and race are not synonymous with problems, with deprivation. They can be sources of great joy and communal strength. Class and race, in this society, however, are manipulated markers of privilege and power. Ms. Hampton had a vision of what life should be; it was a grand, simple vision, filled with good friends and good food, a warm home and her lover by her side. She gave all she could to doing the best she could. The sorrow is in the fact that she and so many others have had to work so hard for such basic human territory.

"I wish you knew what it's like to be me" is the challenge posed by a society divided by race and class. We have so much to learn about one another's victories, the sweetnesses as well as the losses. By expanding our models for what makes a life lesbian or what is a lesbian moment in history, we will become clearer about contemporary political and social coalitions that must be forged to ensure all our liberations.

We are just beginning to understand how social constructs shape lesbian and gay lives. We will have to change our questions and our language of inquiry to take our knowledge deeper. Class and race, always said together as if they meant the same thing, may each call forth their own story. The insights we gain will anchor our other discussions in the realities of individual lives, reminding us that bread and roses, material survival and cultural identity, are the starting points of so many of our histories.

In that spirit, I will always remember our Friday-night dinners at the archives, with a life-size photograph of Gertrude Stein propped up at one end of the table; Ms. Hampton sitting across from Lee Hudson; Denver, the family dog, right at Ms. Hampton's elbow; and myself, looking past the candlelight to my two dear friends, Lee and Mabel—each of us carrying different histories, joined by our love and need for one another.

Ms. Hampton's address at the 1984 New York City Gay Pride rally:

I, Mabel Hampton, have been a lesbian all my life, for eighty-two years, and I am proud of myself and my people. I would like all my people to be free in this country and all over the world, my gay people and my black people.

A Fragile Union

The songs quoted or echoed here come from the thirty-fifth edition of a small red book entitled IWW Songs–To Fan the Flames of Discontent, which was first handed out to would-be union members in 1909.

She stood in front of us, holding her clipboard close to her full breasts, counting us off as we settled into our seats. We had another long bus trip ahead of us, from the gates of this lonely college deep in Flushing, New York, to a Senate meeting room in Washington, D.C. I always felt secure when Carol was in charge. A daughter of labor organizers who had paid dearly for their dreams in the red-hating forties, she was a captivating combination of Emma Goldman and Molly Goldberg. Carol led us into political action with a fierce sense of organization that made us feel invincible. When Carol was in charge, the spit never hit us; the invectives lost their sting.

Solidarity forever, solidarity forever,
solidarity forever,
for the Union makes us strong.

"Subversives" is what some in this country called us, what they called those who traveled on endless early-morning bus trips, walked endless miles, tirelessly handing out the leaflets that called attention to a social wrong. I was lucky enough, gloriously lucky, to have found my way to their encampment, to have had the chance to see the early-morning sunlight hit the ever-hopeful aged faces of the women who had grown old in the movement, who in their sixties and seventies could not be deterred from marching once again. In 1959, in her matronly yet combative stance, Carol became for me the younger face of this determined courage.

Carol stood, swaying slightly, as the bus lurched its way down the avenue, her blouse tucked neatly into her tweed skirt, her slightly heeled pumps adding to her authority over us. When she turned to speak to the driver, bending slightly, the skirt pulled over her hips, forming that rounded, controlled curve for which girdles were invented. This is my first lesbian memory of Carol, the first time her body broke through the political armor she wore into my own body. This image marks a decade for me: the curve of a woman's hip in 1959, controlled by a man-made garment. I think of that curve now with all its contradictions—Carol held in a latex tightness, while she fought for freedom—but at the time I simply sat in the darkened bus and wondered at the desire that flooded me.

Carol was straight, the steady date of Mike, another grown-up veteran of the red-baiting days, who had sultry lips and a slightly muscled body. So I remained a follower, an admirer from afar, a foot soldier in this small army going full tilt against the vestiges of the McCarthy era. The others, Carol and Mike and Carl and Howard, knew the words to all the anthems that had once called people together to form an international movement for a classless, warless world. From them, I learned to sing those songs, and I believed, perhaps even more deeply than they did, in the power of those melodies to carry us forward to a new day.

I also traveled by night, to places whose history was not yet written, to the dark bars that paled before the marble columns of national capitals. In these years, my secret was not my support of socialism, nor my resistance to nuclear arms, nor my battle against the House Un-American Activities Committee. My secret lay deeper, in the recesses of butch-fem communities, in the other subversive life I lived, where only women touched women. Here I journeyed–here, where police and social hatred formed a hard crust around our erotic territories. By the mid-sixties, I was a full citizen of these two tainted communities, living in the neighborhood of immigrants, the Lower East Side. From my small, dilapidated apartment on East Sixth Street, I ventured forth to join my comrades by day and my lovers by night.

My political comrades were curious about my apartment. Not only was I the first woman of our group to be living on my own, but rumors of my sexual deviation had floated back to them. Over the ensuing years, I learned that while my friends spoke passionately of the class struggle, most of them kept close to their middle-class harbors. My queer life on a dark avenue below Fourteenth Street had dramatic appeal. This is how Carol came to me. After one political meeting that lasted late into the night, she asked if she could come over to see my place.

The apartment had no saving graces. A large hole gaped in the ceiling; the thin walls carried my neighbors' screams of frustration, of despair. The cries of babies, already living under the curse of hopeless anger, pierced whatever peace I found there. Living on Sixth Street was not a chosen adventure; it was the place I had to live, the place I could afford.

> The banks are made of marble
> with a guard at every door
> and the vaults are stuffed with silver
> that the workers sweated for.

The walk to my apartment was short, but I panted with nervousness. Carol tapped alongside me, still wearing her small heels, her skirt, her hair done up in the same tight twist she had worn on all those bus rides. We climbed the four flights of tenement stairs, narrow, crumbling steps that led us to floors soaked in years of human habitation. When I was alone, I did not romanticize my street, but now, leading the way for this properly dressed woman–I always saw Carol as a woman, while my own gender slipped and slid all over the place–I was proud of my battered territory.

The apartment itself had only one room with two windows facing the street. A couch under the windows, a fold-out bed, and a desk were the major pieces of furniture. A galley kitchen ran down one side of the room. On the walls I had hung the inexpensive reproductions that museums had waiting for students who had just discovered the wonders of art. Picasso's *Guernica* arched over my desk.

Kicking off her shoes, Carol made herself comfortable on the couch, drawing her nyloned legs up under her, while I poured us both small tumblers of Scotch.

"What is it like, being a lesbian?" she ventured, as I sat down beside her.

Now I held the clipboard, but my acute sense of her body, wrapped in its functional clothing, robbed me of any authority. I talked, words came out, but touch, the need to touch, was a shimmering presence over me. She had led me into battle, but now, I thought, now there is no enemy. Even today, as I try to make a story of this memory, I feel lost in my desire for her, for the touch of her blouse against my cheek, for her hand on my breast. She was not expected; she came, I thought, as a gift.

I was lying with my head on her lap. She had unpinned her hair. The words had stopped. I was no longer afraid but joyous at the feel of her thighs beneath my head, her breasts within reach of my mouth.

"I always just wanted to do one thing," she said, bending over me so her hair veiled my face.

"Do it," I said. She bent down and kissed me. I remember a long, deep kiss, with my heart breaking at the impossibility of it. I remember her tongue full in my mouth, my hand going up to the back of her neck. I wanted to hold it all in place. Only one kiss, only one time of touch.

"You are so soft, so soft," she murmured, as her breath touched my face.

I want to tell you more, to extend the poised moment into years of feeling. I want this moment in this story to have no ending, to have no loss.

But what I do remember next is touched with endings. Carol stands, fixing her hair, pulling it back into its French roll, replacing the bobby pins with determined jabs, bending a little so she can see her face more clearly in the small mirror. I stand behind her. She is speaking to me, to my image in the mirror, with a bobby pin gripped between her lips, her hands competently swirling her hair back into place.

"You know," she says, her eyes locking onto mine in the mirror, "you must never tell anyone about this."

My hands, poised to rest on her shoulders, dropped to my side. All we had been through together, all the shouts and tiredness, all the fear and exuberance, all the hope and anger, froze into loss.

I watched her put herself back together again. This was not the first time I had stood before this mirror caught in its reflections. A few months earlier, Paul, a man who wanted to be my lover, had sneered at me as I put lipstick on in front of this same mirror. "Who are you kidding?" he said. None of this made sense to me. I was young. Why couldn't I want to feel beautiful, why couldn't I speak about a kiss? I knew the world outside thought I was ugly and immoral, but this was my home and these were my friends. I was young and wanted both the beauty of the moment and the passion of my sex.

That was the last time I saw Carol. The sixties swept me up, and I learned other songs of liberation, rode on other buses, found new comrades with the light upon their faces. But I had learned my lesson and kept my touch close to my side. Solidarity is not forever; it shatters on the rocks of difference, on the fear of exile. But passion burns a place in memory, reserving for itself an inner life, biding its time, waiting for reclamation. Songs still fed a movement's dreams, and I was honored to sing them as we marched along, but my life was a secret.

> This little light of mine,
> I'm going let it shine, let it shine.

Songs, like our bodies, carry history in a fragile yet enduring way. Made of breath and born of flesh, they ask us to remember the sweetnesses that once they brought and the strength that once they gave. I have lived long enough now to know what I must sing about, and so I claim this kiss.

The Will to Remember: My Journey with the Lesbian Herstory Archives

      The most searing reminder of our colonized world was the bathroom line. Now I know it stands for all the pain and glory of my time, and I carry that line and the women who endured it deep within me. Because we were labeled deviants, our bathroom habits had to be watched. Only one woman at a time was allowed into the toilet because we could not be trusted. Thus the toilet line was born, a twisting horizon of lesbian women waiting for permission to urinate, to shit.

      The line flowed past the far wall, past the bar, the front room tables, and reached into the back room. Guarding the entrance to the toilet was a short, square, handsome butch woman, the same one every night, whose job it was to twist around her hand our allotted amount of toilet paper. She was us, an obscenity, doing the man's tricks so we could breathe. The line awaited all of us every night, and we developed a line act. We joked, we cruised, we commented on the length of time one of us took, we made special pleas to allow hot-and-heavy lovers in together, knowing full well that our lady would not permit it. I stood a fem, loving the women on either side of me, loving my comrades for their style, the power of their stance, the hair hitting the collar, the thrown-out hip, the hand encircling the beer can. Our eyes played the line, subtle touches, gentle shyness weaved under the blaring jokes, the music, the surveillance. We lived on that line; restricted and judged, we took deep breaths and played.

But buried deep in our endurance was our fury. That line was practice and theory seared into one. We wove our freedoms, our culture, around their obstacles of hatred, but we also paid our price. Every time I took the fistful of toilet paper, I swore eventual liberation. It would be, however, liberation with a memory.

– "The Bathroom Line," *A Restricted Country*

For the marginalized, remembering is an act of will, a conscious battle against ordained emptiness. For gay people, remembering is an act of alchemy–the transformation of dirty jokes, limp wrists, a wetted pinky drawn over the eyebrow into bodies loved, communities liberated. When Albert Memmi wrote the following passage in 1967, he was speaking as a Tunisian Jew who had an intimate understanding of both cultural exile and cultural power:

The colonized draw less and less from their past. The colonizer never even recognized that they had one; everyone knows that the commoner whose origins are unknown has no history. Let us ask the colonized herself: who are her folk heroes, her great popular leaders, her sages? At most she may be able to give us a few names, in complete disarray and fewer and fewer as one goes down the generations. The colonized seems condemned to lose her memory. *[female pronouns mine.]*

– *The Colonizer and the Colonized*, 1967

When I read those words in 1971, I knew he was speaking for me as well.

The politics of culture is a very complex thing, filled with opportunities for acceptance that can turn in an instant to moments of betrayal of self and community. Deprivation of cultural recognition makes one hungry, makes one yearn for the center. But for those who have lived in a ghetto of any kind, the matter is not one of a simple exchange of marginality for normalization.

In 1992, I was asked to speak at an older women's educational forum at Bryn Mawr College. Three of us from differing backgrounds had been asked to address the themes of diversity, silence, marginality, and danger. I knew I had been asked to be part of this event because of my work with the Lesbian Herstory Archives, and in preparation, I had been scribbling down random thoughts and disturbing excerpts from the daily newspapers, as I usually do when some idea, not yet clearly expressed, is nibbling at my mind. For some time, I had been wondering about what the national concern for diversity actually meant when it applied to gay people. I thought I had found some clues.

From the *New York Times*, March 2, 1992:
Jews Debate the Issue of Gay Clergy Members

From the *New York Times*, April 9, 1992:
The bishops issued the 3rd draft of a Letter on Women calling for lesbians to practice chastity.

From the same newspaper, April 12, 1992:
Examples abound of subjects that were very much discussed by insiders [on the pro-tennis circuit] but publicly taboo, ranging from the gay subculture on the women's tour to drug abuse on the men's. No one wanted to spread scandal.

While I applauded the concern with diversity, these ongoing cultural skirmishes made me suspicious. How does a woman who has lived her life as what most societies, including this one, call a "sexual deviant" leave the cultural place that has been her home for over forty years? How does she decide what to take with her and what to leave behind? What to remember and what to forget? For this is the challenge we face when we are asked to believe that the society around us is really changing, that marginal voices are being asked to join a chorus of equitable inclusion.

As a queer woman–and I use that term because I came to my sexual and cultural self in the working-class bars of Greenwich Village in the 1950s and '60s and there I was schooled in queer survival–I am not convinced that the calls for inclusion really include me or my community, in our full cultural expression. I could pass as a woman, even as a feminist–though respect for this profound way of seeing the world is getting more difficult to come by–but as a lesbian who insists on the importance of her sexual choices, I do not feel on safe ground. I know how to live on the shifting terrain of the margin, for there we knew more than the intruders, but I move very cautiously into the new territory that is being offered.

Perhaps younger women will feel more at ease, more trusting of this new place, but they will not have the same memories, the same fears of betrayal, the same sense of comrades left at the border who could not cross over. How do I remain true to Maria, the bartender from Barcelona, who protected me from police entrapment in the early 1960s, or to Rachel, the lesbian whore who lay in my arms dreaming of a kinder world, or the butch women I saw stripped by the police in front of their lovers? These actions happened in marginal places, the reserves on which we were allowed to touch or dance or strut until someone decided enough of these freaks and took our fragile freedom away.

But this old country, as Baldwin called his historical ghetto– the Jim Crow–ridden American South–is a complex and paradoxical place. I never want my lesbian daughters to have to find each other in bars where police brutality is rampant, to dance in a public place where a bouncer measures the distance between the partners to make sure no parts of the body are touching. I never want their clitoris and nipples measured by doctors convinced that lesbians are hormonal abnormalities, as was done in the 1930s and '40s, and yet, while I know that living in the preliberation gay ghetto endangered my life, remembering it *gives* me life.

My journey with the Lesbian Herstory Archives can be told in two ways—the factual development of a vision into a building filled with the artifacts of lesbian life or the interior movement from my sense as a person deprived of historical memory to one glorying in the possibility of it. The journey from deprivation into plentitude is how I have put it on endless archives tours. It is also a journey from silence into speech, from shame into revelation.

From the archives' visitors' book, 1979:
For two days I have been thinking up wise and pithy things that I should include—no dice. So perhaps, the honest will work better. Only once before have I felt like I've come home. This is the second time. I never thought I would be that lucky again—and I realize it is my right to come home to the world. Thanks to you and all the lives in this room for showing me that right!
– Judy

One of the first cultural goals of the archives project was to salvage secrets, to stop the destruction of letters and photographs, to rescue the documents of our desire from family and cultural devaluation. At almost every presentation of the archives slide show, a woman would tell us a tale of loss, of a family member destroying diaries or burning letters. Time and time again a woman would confide in us how she had destroyed records of her early homoerotic life, whether it was her stash of 1950s lesbian paperbacks, the first cultural products she had ever found that testified to a public lesbian world, or the passionate outpourings of young love. I will never forget the moments of understanding that occurred, of relief and sometimes of mourning, when an older woman accepted the possibility that acts she had considered shameful for so long could be seen in another way, could be seen as cherished cultural moments in a community's history. In the early 1970s, this acceptance of another context for the remembered touch was a pure act of will.

In the early years of the archives, Deborah Edel and I scoured small-town library and church book-sale tables, often finding a rare lesbian novel that had been selected for throwaway; in the mail, we would often get posters and other memorabilia that had been saved from trash heaps. So many times did this reversal of cultural fortune happen that we publicly spoke about transforming what this society considered garbage into a people's history. The retrieved documents in their often coded and yet staunch way challenge the prevailing historical view of the pathology of same sex-love. Now I understand that these acts of retrieval were also personal moments of reconstitution for me.

An excerpt from a love letter (c. 1920) found in a Greenwich Village gutter after the family had cleaned out the apartment of Eleanor C., a labor educator of the thirties and forties:

This is a "very quiet" letter, Eleanor dear, and you won't read it when you are dashing off somewhere in a hurry, will you–please.

Thursday night
Best Beloved
I'm writing by the light of the two tall candles on my desk, with the flamey chrysanthemums you arranged before me. It's such a lovely soft glow and I'm glad because this is a "candle light" letter. I wish you could know what a wonderful person you are, Eleanor darling, and what joy your letter written last night gave me. Not the part about me–that is pitifully wrong and only a standard for me to measure up to–but

you make it all so wonderful and are clear about it all, but I could never say so, even in incoherent fashion, and so many times back of my nobler resolves I am just plain selfish about wanting you to look at and talk to— and I'm not afraid dear, I know our love will help—oh so much and not hinder, it never does that, not even in my weakest moments....

The candles are burning low, dear heart and the world is very still and beautiful outside. And I am so, oh so happy that I know you and love you. May God bless you through all time.

– Alice

My history with the growth of the archives directly parallels my involvement with gay liberation and lesbian feminism. Just as my queer past was constructed by social judgments and culturally restrictive politics, my time of hope was hewn out of the glory of public possibilities. The early 1970s, so deeply influenced by the progressive movements of the '60s, was a time when some constructed a new social self.

In 1972, a few of us who worked in or were being educated by the City University system of New York, people like Martin Duberman and Seymour Kleinberg, founded an organization called the Gay Academic Union (GAU). This was how we did things back then. If there was a problem of lesbian or gay exclusion or misrepresentation, we sat down in a circle and came up with an organization to address it. Concerned with the plight of gay students and teachers in high schools and colleges, the GAU became a rallying place for early gay scholarship and battles against isolation and homophobia in the educational system.

The Lesbian Herstory Archives was conceived in discussions with members of my GAU consciousness-raising group, women like Deborah Edel, who was to become my first lesbian-feminist lover as well as co-founder of the archives; Julia Penelope Stanley, whom I had known in the "old" days and whose version of radical feminism I would come to vehemently oppose; her lover Sahli; and Pamela, a political lesbian. Here in an embryonic form were the streams of consciousness of the '70s, ranging from old-time fem to gay liberation politics to lesbian separatism to "lesbian" as a political identification without erotic significance. And here also was the beginning of the discourse about memory, history, and sexuality that would keep me in its throes for the next thirty years. In the archives' statement of purpose, our need for cultural autonomy rings out loud and clear.

From the archives' newsletter, no. 1, 1975:

The Lesbian Herstory Archives exists to gather and preserve records of lesbian lives and activities so that future generations will have ready access to materials relevant to their lives. The process of gathering this material will also serve to uncover and collect our herstory denied to us previously by patriarchal historians in the interests of the culture which they serve. The existence of these archive will enable us to analyze and reevaluate the lesbian experience; we also anticipate that the existence of these archives will encourage lesbians to record their experiences in order to formulate our living herstory.

The archives, with its collection of lesbians speaking for themselves in a myriad of ways, was to be our answer to the medical, legal, and religious colonization of our lives. In 1974, the Lesbian Herstory Archives took up its home in the large apartment I shared with Deborah Edel. My relationship with Deborah was a living symbol of the archives' cultural compassion; she, shaped by the 1970s, never flinched at my tales of the bars, at my need to find the voices and images of the community that had given me life and to make sure that the artifacts of this earlier lesbian time had a home.

The generosity of Deborah's historical and psychological imagination allowed me to work out ways to give a place of honor to life I had lived on the margins of American society, while we worked to change the norms of that same society by creating the very notion of lesbian and gay history. I used the archives' newsletter to express my concern about the kind of history we were about to create and to do battle with the more severe lesbian feminists who were so judgmental of my preliberation butch-fem community. Using all the tools of liberatory politics, I was attempting to hold on to a place I knew of as home and to let it go all at the same time.

From the archives' newsletter, no. 7, 1981:

If we ask decorous questions of history, we will get a genteel history. If we assume that because sex was a secret, it did not exist, we will get a sexless history. If we assume that in periods of oppression, lesbians lost their autonomy and acted as victims only, we destroy not only history but lives. For many years, the psychologists told us we were both emotionally and physically deviant; they measured our nipples and clitorises to chart our queerness, they talked about how we wanted to be men and how our sexual styles were pathetic imitations of the real thing and all along under this barrage of hatred and fear, we loved. They told us that we should hate ourselves and sometimes we did, but we were also angry, resilient and creative. And most of all, were lesbian women, revolutionizing each of these terms.

We create history as much as we discover it. What we call history becomes history and since this is a naming time, we must be on guard against our own class prejudices and discomforts. If close friends and devoted companions are to be part of lesbian history, so must be also the lesbians of the fifties who left no doubt about their sexuality or their courage.

Because of my own experience with the criminalizing 1950s, I felt it was essential that the archives not become a hand-picked collection of respectable lesbian role models. This emphasis on inclusiveness made the archives a focus of controversy. Yes, we wanted the papers of Samois, the first national public lesbian S/M group. Yes, we wanted the diary of a lesbian prostitute. Yes, we would cherish the pasties of a lesbian stripper. Yes, we wanted collections of woman-with-woman pornography. I knew that a memory fashioned to the prevailing precepts of one time, no matter how profound that time may be, would never be complex enough, never filled with wonders enough, to be the living, needed gift to the unknown future that we all wanted this collection to be.

Now hard hats and hobnail boots sit next to pasties and glossy prints of a famous lesbian stripper of the 1940s. They, in turn, are joined by the Lavender Menace T-shirt of the NOW rebellion in the 1970s; photographs of bar patrons of the 1930s are in the same room as images from the Michigan Womyn's Music Festival. A DOB (Daughters of Bilitis) certificate of organization, an artifact from the late 1950s, shares a shelf with a Lesbian Avengers poster, an artifact from the urban 1990s. A copy of "Women-Loving Women," the manifesto of the early days of lesbian feminism, lies next to an album cover featuring the smiling, boyish face of Billy Tipton, the jazz musician who was born a woman but passed as a man for most of his life. This is the history I wanted: a conversation of possibilities, of lineages, of contradictions.

Throughout my intimate life with the archives, for the twenty years or so that it filled my apartment with its file cabinets and book-shelves, its endless stream of visitors, I was always looking for icons of resistance. I found them in the out-of-print books, the oral history tapes, old copies of homophile publications like *Vice-Versa* and *The Ladder*, snapshots, and snatches of conversation between visitors. Stories came to me–the story of the young butch woman in the 1950s who always sewed a piece of lace on her socks before she went to the bars so the police would not arrest her for transvestism, the story of the sophisticated fem who carried her dildo in a satin purse so when she left the bar with her chosen woman of the night, she knew the woman would be well pleased, the story of the young Jewish woman who had read *The Well of Loneliness* in Polish before she was taken into the concentration camps. "That book helped me to survive; I wanted to live long enough to kiss a woman," she told me one night while we sat at my dining-room table having a cup of tea. These stories filled my heart; they healed and educated me and changed for me forever that which I would call history. They have become the tropes of my writing, the proclamations of the lesbian spirit that I repeat over and over. They are my jewels of discovery, the riches that lay beneath that marginalized land.

From the archives' newsletter, no. 3, 1976:

Summer was an interesting time for the archives with a record number of visitors including women from California, England and Italy. I found that whether I was talking with lesbians from Manhattan or Europe, the concern expressed for the preservation of our herstory creates an energy that whisks the archives from the past into our daily lives. There is motivation and activity everywhere. In London, women are producing street theater in the Punch and Judy tradition to support the Wages for Housework Campaign. In Italy, lesbian groups are beginning to meet in the high schools. Some of our visitors organized lesbian centers or were responsible for coordinating such notable events as the Lesbian Herstory Exploration near Los Angeles. Of course in many cases the enthusiasm was closer to home, taking the shape of a "Hello, I just found out that the archives is a few blocks away and I'd like to stop by tomorrow." This summer brought a feeling of universal lesbian power—women united in the celebration and adventure of pursuing our identity.
– Valerie

After Deborah and I separated, and Judith Schwarz, who had become part of the archives collective in the late 1970s, moved out of the apartment, I was left alone with this huge collection of memory, in which the past and present sat cheek-to-cheek with each other. I felt this aloneness particularly after Thursday night work groups, when the many women who volunteered to work with the collection would take their leave, several rushing off to the subways and buses that carried them to Brooklyn.

I would walk through the apartment, past the boxes and piles of clippings, wondering at what my life had become. Could these gathered voices keep my own alive? Could these tales of resistance and desperation, of love and the loss of it, of gender construction and sexual adventuring change forever the loneliness of our cultural exile? Of my own life?

> From the visitors' book, 1983:
> I am here among women
> who breathe softly in my ear
> who speak gently
> in a voice that will not be stilled.
> I am here in a cradle
> or a womb,
> or a lap,
> on a knee that is shapely
> under my thigh
> leaving the impression
> that I will never be alone.
>
> I am here
> to remember faces
> I have never seen before
> and I do
> Love,
>
> – Jewelle Gomez

Twenty-nine years have passed since I started this journey to find a public face for lesbian memory. When I look over the archives' newsletters of the 1970s, I can see how the discourse has changed. The word *identity*, so popular in that decade, is more complicated now, more challenged in its implications. Transgender and passing women's history is no longer an orphan child of the movement, and no one need apologize any longer for an interest in butch-fem or leather communities–at least within the confines of our own queer movement. Lesbian, gay, bisexual, and transfolk history are now thriving concerns, with both public and private institutions undertaking their own collections. The success of queer theory on college campuses has ensured, at least for now, a continuing flow of published and cultural discussion. When the New York Public Library opened its gay and lesbian history exhibit a few years ago in a cocktail-party atmosphere, I knew another time had come, and I feared for the life of my grassroots dream.

As I toured the exhibit, one to which the Lesbian Herstory Archives had contributed, I kept thinking of the first time I had ever tried to find out about my queer self. I was a high school senior, and I wanted to do a research paper on homosexuality. The year was 1957. My teacher had told us about the world-renowned library on Fifth Avenue, so I made my way to the institution guarded by its two ageless stone lions. Too ashamed to ask a librarian about my topic, I toured the endless rows of wooden card catalogue cabinets until I found the letter H. I pulled out the long narrow drawer and flipped through the timeworn cards. Finally, my heart beating, I found the word "Homosexual," followed by a dash and then the words "see Deviancy," and next to this "see Pathology," with suggested subcategories of prisons and mental institutions. I never wrote that paper. But years later, remembering that journey of self-hatred and strengthened by my marginalized culture, I helped to create in the same institution that had played such a powerful role in our cultural disenfranchisement another story of same sex-love, one that recognized not only our humanity but also our power of choice, of self-determination.

In 1993 the archives moved into a three-story limestone building in the Park Slope section of Brooklyn, New York. Over two hundred volunteers, including lesbian architects and carpenters, worked for a year to prepare the building for its new life. The core group of coordinators who are responsible for the daily life of the collection has expanded to include over twenty women, many of whom are archivists and librarians. In June of 1996, we celebrated with our larger communities the burning of our mortgage, the accomplishment of a grassroots miracle. I am no longer the caretaker of the collection; I no longer sit at the endless bimonthly meetings where women slosh through the grinding demands of tours, research questions, collection building, workdays. When I can, I take a car service to this Brooklyn home, and I sometimes have to ask a woman I do not know what she is doing or where something is.

After giving a tour, when the house is silent, I walk through the collection. I look into closets to see if old friends are still there—like the army uniform worn by a lesbian woman who served in Vietnam as a medic or the ripped leather jacket with studs on the back, spelling out "Dyketactics," the name of an early zap protest group from Philadelphia. I push a book back into place, or stare into the face of a friend who now lives beyond her death in this home of memory. And I know that sometime I, too, will be returned to where I came from, to this place of cherished difference. When I close the door behind me, I often just stand on the stoop, marveling at the solidity of the home we have created.

And solid it had better be.

From the *New York Times*, July 7, 1998:

Mr. Craig, the organizer of Greenville, South Carolina's Citizens for Traditional Family Values, said he believed that homosexuality was "demonic" and "a stench in the nostrils of God."

Regina at the Races

The Starting Gate, 1910

I remember as a little girl, the impatience I felt with my own youth. I recognized that I was someone to be reckoned with. I sensed the sexual order of life. I wanted to be quickly and passionately involved. I recognized my youth only in the physical sense, as when I looked at my own body, saw the beautiful breasts, the flat stomach, the sturdy limbs, the piquant face, the eyes that had sadness, needed love—a hell of a lot of grit and already an acknowledgment that this was going to be one hell of a life. I knew the hunger but I did not know how to appease it. I was going to find the key.

– Regina Nestle, from her ledger sheets journal, 1972

New York City, 1950

The bus was already packed full with the regulars. "C'mon, let's get this buggy going."

"What's a matter? You can't wait to lose your money?"

"My last horse is still running."

My mother pulled me along, her pocketbook tucked firmly under her arm. I jumped up the steps and rushed to find two seats.

The driver gunned the motor as my mother climbed in.

"Hey, Regina, you're late today."

"Yeah, let's get this show on the road, c'mon, lady."

"Here Regina, sit down next to me," a sandy-haired, red-faced man half rose from his seat, brushing crumbs from his lap. "I need your help."

My mother looked around, trying to spot me. I had found a seat right next to the toilet cabin. I waved to her, giving her permission to sit wherever she wanted. My attention was taken by the busload of passengers, most of whom seemed to know each other. I was surrounded by old men who, like tired scholars, held folded, tattered papers in their hands. My mother was the only woman on the bus, but as soon as she settled into her seat, she blended right in.

I stood up to get a better view and watched as she pulled a well-studied racing form out of her bag. "Here Sam, this is the one I like. I figured the odds, they haven't let this nag win in three races, he's due."

"You're the bookkeeper, you know those numbers," Sam laughed.

The man sitting behind them leaned over the back of Sam's seat. "What you cookin' up today, Regina?"

"How to steal our money back. I could drive those horses better than some of those bozos. Did you see the fifth race last night? McKay practically begged that horse to break. He was holding her back so hard, I thought he was going to break her neck. They must think we are blind fools."

A lurch of the bus as it picked up speed threw me back into my seat. For the rest of the trip, I had a good view of staggering men going to relieve themselves. Cigarette and cigar smoke curled up out of almost every seat as the passengers gave the trotters a piece of their mind. Pencils moved, pages turned, voices rose and fell, hard barks of derision mixed with pleas for help.

"Got any good leads?"

"Sparrow's Song in the third, trust me."

"Hey Kelly, did you walk away with anything last night?"

"Yeah, a stomachache."

I kept a sharp ear out for my mother's voice.

Regina says,

My memory serves me right.

My mother was a large woman who wasn't afraid of anything. She was the peacemaker. Not only in our family but in the neighborhood. I remember holding tight to her hand as she went from peddler to peddler climbing the hills of 135th Street, looking for the best fruit she could find. Once an argument broke out between a Jewish peddler and an Italian customer. My mother imposed her large body between the two screaming men. In her soothing voice, she spoke a little in Yiddish, a little in Italian until peace was made.

When I came home after the rape, she silenced my father with a look. When we were alone, she asked me if I was alright, told me if I was pregnant, I would not be alone, kissed me, and told me to go to bed. Never again was the incident mentioned. But I lost her, too soon. Sadie died of a heart attack in 1935.

No photographs of this woman, yet I smell the camphor in her black dress–heavy, long, rustling with work. Leo, Walter, Jeannette, Regina, Miriam, Carrie–six surviving children out of nine births. Children gathered around her skirts; she was a pioneer woman in the plains of upper Manhattan. Facing outward, turning her body to fend off the wolves, the winters, the hunger, the father. Without her, the children fled each other.

> *My father, Elias, was a drunk and a gambler. His anger ruled the house. We children tiptoed around his tantrums. He would sit, pounding on the kitchen table, screaming at the beer wagons thundering down the hill outside our windows, the horses trying to stay ahead of the plunging wagons. The one man I knew, the one I had access to. He was a flat surface, no dimensions. He ate, he gambled, he never reached out except to touch my breasts once or twice. A loving fatherly gesture. He was on the make.*

Miriam was Regina's twin sister who sometimes joined her on the beach at Coney Island. She was shy about being seen in public; the polio epidemic of the early years of the twentieth century had shrunk her left leg, lifting her instep into a curve that made walking difficult. Sadie, their mother, had spent hours every night massaging Miriam's weakened leg, trying to coax it back to life, while Regina, the stronger twin, stood watching in the doorway. The mystery was how the virus chose one of the girls and not the other, when they always slept in the same bed. The family members spent hours discussing the angel of death and how he made his choices.

I have an old photograph of them—the two sisters—tinted by a Brooklyn artist's hand, their heads leaning on each other, their arms around each other's shoulders, my mother's arm hanging at her side, my aunt's hand poised coyly at her hip. Black-and-white broad vertical stripes run down their identical bathing suits, which reach to their middle thighs. The picture is cut off at the knees, but even so you can see the narrowing of my aunt's leg. That is how I know for sure she is Miriam and not

Regina. She is smiling, my mother is not. Behind them are the torsos of prone female bodies and part of a beach umbrella; right between them, I can see the lower portion of a man, fully dressed, white shirt, black pants with a belt. The camera has caught him taking a step, his leather shoe pointing to my mother's hip.

> Regina remembers:
> *Rockaway, 1924*
> *A gaudy summer resort. I was there to take care of my older sister's child. The deserted beach was my retreat. The ocean was my savior. I could see a great span of space. The horizon was my hope, my escape, no buffeting, no challenging. I knew loneliness, always knew it, so when this beautiful young man came to sit by me, in the evening twilight with the beach deserted, he unknowingly joined me in my quest.*
> *He was about twenty-five, curly hair, blue eyes, stocky build, good-looking. "A pretty girl alone. How come?"*
> *"Just watching," my voice muted. The challenge had come—a young man was seeing me. I watched myself as a warmth crept over my body. My dimples were showing. I thrust my body forward to accentuate the outline of my breasts. I was going to make it.*

The smell of the beach, the acrid tang of seaweed and broken sea flesh, a Brooklyn beach now empty but on the weekends filled with men in cotton bathing suits and women in broadly stripped suits that come down to their knees. The shouts of children, the rushes of young men as they threaten their dates with dunking in the always-cold sea. Smells of frankfurters and pastrami, sauerkraut and borscht, beer kept cold buried deep in the sand, broken bits of dreams that bite at the naked heels of beach walkers.

The Party, 1924

One night about two months later, he invited me to a party. I went with fear, not trusting the man I loved. Yes, I thought I was in love. At fourteen, that is easy to do, to fall in love with a promise.

You know the saying, when you had one, you have had them all—well that was what happened to me that night. He passed me on to his friends, three in all. I did not move. I disconnected myself from my body, froze my mind. I am sure I was a lousy lay. After it was all over, he took me to my door at six in the morning. Not a word did I say. My father and mother were waiting. My father started to call me all the vile words he knew in English. My mother quietly stated that she controlled the children. She would mete out the punishment if necessary. I walked by them, went into the room I shared with Miriam and pulled the blanket over my head. The next day I left school and found a job in a furrier's office.

Beaver, chinchilla, mink, ermine, fox, mouton lamb, rabbit, sable, seal, sea otter.

Regina wonders about her guilt:

Doctor, this one experience now haunts me and I seek the answer. Was I the victim or the stimulus of the event? That evening of the rape I came away still young, still desiring the beauty of a sexual relationship, frightened that words could not express the experience, afraid to admit that there existed in men such cruelty. I buried the truth. I lived the lie that men do not and cannot perpetuate evil. Love is all. But in my life, despair took over.

Plucking, shearing, bleaching, dyeing.

The Furrier's Office, 1924

The smell of worked hide, the glistening fur, fox and beaver, sleek with fats and oils. Regina gets glimpses of this richness only when she goes to the ladies' room, passing the long room with men in white shirt sleeves rolled back to their elbows, cutting the peltries to fit the chalk outlines of the desired garment. Wetting, slitting, stretching, stitching skin to skin, skin to design. Fanned out, the shaped hides are pinned to the board; hundreds of long metal pins, like railroad spikes, fasten the beaver and the lamb, the fox and the mink to their destinies. When a buyer comes in from out of town, the girls are called in to model the jackets and coats, the finished products of those tables. Little jackets with fox heads at their necks, full-length minks that swing from the girls' shoulders. The buyers, men with cigars, reach for the hemlines, rolling the fur between their fingers, touching the smooth legs of the girls. Regina learned to be a bookkeeper, but she was always watching.

Run, Regina, run.

The Furrier's Office, 1927

Three years of learning her trade, smelling, touching, counting the piles of animal skins, growing impatient with life. One night, Jonas, a good-looking young man who works as a cutter, pushes her down onto a pile of furs, and they lie there, talking. He touches her breast, his hand squeezing and pushing, his thumb making circles around her nipple. She fights to have feeling, wanting to drown out the night when the sea betrayed her. Her mouth tastes of cigarettes and pickle, but she allows him to put his tongue inside. Suddenly she is sucking like a baby, wanting more and more of him. Her hands wrap around his shoulders, pull at his white shirt. She feels his hardness through his pants. She will have to be careful so he doesn't find out that she is damaged goods. She wants this–the penis and the vagina. Life is all in her now, her breasts are strong, her belly is ready. Jonas will be her husband. But he will never

know that four men took her body's first free yearning and drowned it in
the sea.

Regina says,
Identity is where you find it.

The sounds of small animals scratching in the underbrush,
licking their paws, cleaning their fur, preening, pawing. Jonas wanted
this young woman, on their bed of fur, this girl with a hint of the flapper
to her. All day he worked with fur, slicing the skin so he could mold the
pelt to the shape of a cape, of a coat. Late in the afternoon, he floated
above the table, smelling the perfume of the women who would wear the
finished piece, feeling their breath full of gratitude on his cheeks, the rus-
tle of their gowns. The small animals scratching and nibbling, holding
live things in their immaculate paws.

The twenty-four-year-old Jonas moved his hand under
Regina's skirt, feeling his way into her body. As he pushed aside the wet
panties, his fingers finding fur, she caught his hand. Enough was enough,
she pretended.

Only a short time did the young furrier and his wife have
together. Enough to establish who was boss. Regina would sneak up to
the roof to smoke, an act her husband did not approve of. He never knew
about the rape. When he was thirty-nine, the angel of death decided
enough was enough.

Regina asserts,
So many splinters and yet not broken.
Joe's death was quick, painful, and not merciful. He wanted to
live: he was young, vital, had a son he adored and a wife that
sufficed. He tried so hard to survive, and when we parted at
the hospital, knowing he could not make it, he asked me how

I was going to manage. I told him to let go. I would make it,
but more important, his child and the child to come surely
would. The last words between two who had created life. Joan
was born five months later, and in those five months, all values,
all images of family, of compassion, were destroyed.

Run, Regina, run.

The athletic young man who loved the outdoors and horsing
around with his buddies left this world of furs and teeth, in 1939, leaving
mysteries behind.

April 1969
Upon questioning me further, the doctor elicited the informa-
tion that I had been a widow for twenty-five years. He asked
me if I'd had any sexual relationships during this span. I
looked at him. You haven't enough fingers or toes to count
them.

From the Fur Trade Foundation 1939 Charity Report: one
grant to "a fur man's widow who needed funeral expenses."

Regina faced the war alone. She left the fur traders behind
and moved to the back rooms reserved for bookkeepers in the garment
industry. Junior Togs. Lucky Lady. Bon Dana. Maiden Wear, Vanity Frocks,
Junior Wear. Sportswear. Ladies' Garments. Numbers and words, lovers
and horses, scotch and numbers, children and words, black-market deals
and whores, lovers and household finance, apartments and scotch, lovers
and evictions, children and subpoena, numbers and touch, whore and
mother.

Regina says,

I am silenced, but my silence shall be louder than my words.
The garment industry is run by illusionists, magicians, pan-
derers to the world. The buyers are prostitutes. Give them what
will please their customers, you own them. Displease their
customers, you have lost security. Season after season, I was
part of the cycle, saw the struggle, became part of it, dipped
into the excitement of money, power, physical attraction,
adornment, flattery, sensuality. Sex was like afternoon cock-
tails, the theater tickets, the "black-market" bribery, the procur-
ing of nylons–all trivialities but of paramount importance. If
you had something that someone else could not get, you had it
made. It was easy and pathetic after paying off your first IRS
man. How sometimes I wished they would set me free. You see,
I didn't have the strength to do it myself. I was guilty and so
was the world. It had no values and neither did I, or so it
seemed. I saw less and less of my children. I had a housekeep-
er, efficient. I was with the children on weekends. The total
transition from one world to another began to show its effects.
It became more difficult for me to live. Loneliness became my
friend, and dreams became reality. The war, business, good
food, clothes, even the beauty of the children grew dim.

Bronx, 1953

Ben was a short, squat man, his face coming to a point like a
turtle's. Where my mother first met him, I do not know. Maybe in one of
those buses going to the track.

"Ben's taking us to the track," my mother announced one
night. "Wear something nice."

I had a pink dress, with small white flowers embossed on it,
and a scoop neckline. Like other teenagers of the fifties, I also had the
prerequisite crinoline, a wire hoop that gave a perfect bell shape to the
bottom part of the dress. Whenever I wore that pink and white billowing

creation, I felt like I was going to a ball, a ball in the Bronx.

We went in style to the track that night, in Ben's car, not on the bus. My mother was also dolled up, but she always was when she was out with one of her boyfriends. Even the ones who looked like turtles.

Ben was the only one dressed like he always was. Pants too short clinging to his round stomach. Jacket bunching up at his armpits. Hair slicked down. A cigar in his shirt pocket. A big smile on his face as he squired his "two little ladies" through the entrance gate. I wondered if he was holding my mother's hand as tightly as he was holding mine.

He settled us in the green wooden seats, and my mother began poring over the racing sheets. I had some trouble getting my crinoline to lie flat enough, so I could sit without feeling I was balancing on a spring. As soon as I had found a way to do it, Ben said, "C'mon with me, kid. Let's place a few bets." My mother let us pass with a brief look of annoyance.

As soon as we had left the stands behind, I knew something was up. Ben put his arm around me, pulling me close. "I want to introduce you to the guys," he said. "Here, take my arm." He steered me toward a clump of four or five middle-aged men who started to smirk before we even reached them. "Hey Ben, is that your new girlfriend?"

By now, I was cringing. "Yeah, I like them young," Ben laughed, hugging me to his side, forcing my crinoline into a U-shape. The call to the next race saved me from further embarrassment as the men moved off to place their bets. Ben, still holding my hand, pulled me in another direction. The floor under my feet was sticky with spilled beer and spongy globs of losing tickets. My black patent leather pumps, worn only with this outfit, were quickly losing their shininess.

Somehow Ben managed to find a dark, empty place near one of the stanchions holding up the tiers of seats. All around us were the rush of the crowds, the smells of frankfurters and cigarettes, the noises of thousands of people pushing at their fates, but in that small space, we were alone. Ben backed me against the iron pillar. "I really like how you look tonight. How about giving me a kiss?"

I kept hoping the crinoline, my first line of defense, would hold him off, but it buckled under his forward surge. "Kiss him and get it over with," I thought. His face was two inches from mine. I smiled like a good thirteen-year-old and gave him a quick peck on the cheek.

"No, I mean a real kiss." Ben aimed his turtle face at me and stuck his tongue into my mouth. At the same time, he grabbed my breast, newly adorned in a cotton bra. I didn't know which area to protect first. For one moment, I savored the sensation of what a tongue could feel like in my mouth, storing the information away for later use, while the rest of me roared in protest. Using the iron behind me to give extra leverage, I launched my two arms into his belly, shoving him off me. "Leave me alone!" I screamed. Then I ran, my shoes slipping on the matted debris.

Regina says,
I cannot survive the woman that I am.

In the intervening years between the hot war and the cold war, Regina embezzled money to cover her gambling debts, lost some of her appeal, took more lovers, and in long drunken nights poured her heart onto the ledger sheets she ripped out of the big blue books she kept so well for her bosses. Her last battles were fought to settle scores with her employers and to save her children from the chaos of her life.

October 15, 1976
Mr. Brenner:
I received the subtle threat addressed to my children, with regards to my misdeeds, which, incidentally, you were aware of as far back as two and a half years ago. I did not at any time cover or manipulate your books to hide the deficit. I am not pleading my cause; as a matter of fact, part of my healing is admitting to "improper behavior"—but for you to assume a

*holier-than-thou moral judgment is laughable. The powerful
have the right, your philosophy?*
*Now to the settlement of the debt. There are discrepancies and
I shall enumerate: According to my records, the $800 given
back to you from my bonus seems not to be credited to my
account. I may be in error and the only way this can be proven
is to send copies of my earning sheets of 1974 and 1975, showing deductions from my income to be credited to indebtedness
and judgments against my salary. As to the $60 for dresses
that you list, I paid this sum to your former colleague,
Johnnie, you remember him, your dispenser of checks. Poor
soul, he thought he had it made. Don't we all, including you.
I am sure I am not intimidating you, and it is not my style,
as I am accountable for my actions. As you are for yours.
However, you'd better believe that all correspondence now or
in the future directed to my children shall possibly be a heart-
ache to you. My sins are mine, period.*

From the ledger of Lenox Hill Hospital:
one suitcase
two pair of glasses
one bag of writings
one robe
two books
one pair of slippers
three pairs of pajamas
No valuables
–December 22, 1978, the day Regina died of a heart attack

Regina croons a lullaby that was never heard, August 30, 1965:
Close your eyes, sweet child, let all dreams be true.
May all the blessings of happiness come to you.

Close your eyes, my darling, do not be afraid.
Mother will comfort you, keep you warm.
All dangers cease to be,
When love keeps close watch.
Close your eyes, my darling.
No harm can come to you,
Press your curly head upon my breast.
Your strength you give to me,
This is the source of all the grief,
Close your eyes, my darling, so the tears I shed shall not be seen.

Twenty Years After Regina's Death, 1997

Mother, tonight I can smell you. I can hear the sounds of your girdle and full-line bra being peeled off your body. I can see you standing at attention in the basic black sheath you always wore, a sturdy black column except for the roll of flesh that always escaped the prison of the foundation garments. Why, at fifty-seven, do I remember your body so? Is this the lesbian daughter claiming her desire for her mother, the first woman whose smell meant seduction and loss, security and homeless-ness? Or is it the huge need to touch you, to feel your hand on my arm, comforting me in the face of cancer? Or is it both? And the need to pull you back from the place where you have gone.

I glimpse no harbor and can't see the point of departure.

Regina remembers another bus ride, 1968:
I met him on a bus coming from the track. I was terribly depressed, not because of losing but from the sheer inanity of spending another evening without any personal contact or involvement. He sat down beside me, even though there were many empty seats. Casually glancing at him, I saw a man in his middle forties, strong featured, but most of all, a brooding

face, hunched shoulders, quite a big man. He asked me how I had made out. I told him, indifferently, lost a little.

The conversation became desultory until I heard him say he had just returned from Vietnam. I reacted immediately, wanting to know about conditions, elicited from him that he'd been on a ship delivering war materials. Upon hearing his version of the war, I dubbed him a reactionary–but what the hell, he was someone to talk to. The wildest and most revealing experience of my life began.

We got off the bus at Forty-Second Street, typically lost people with no place to go, when he indifferently asked me if I would care to have a drink. We went to a bar across from where I lived, on the East Side, and I proceeded to get cockeyed drunk. I left myself wide open for whatever would happen. Do I sound unemotional about it all? I had better be. Yes, I knew from the beginning that he was a loner. I knew he needed human contact, but so did I. Thinking that I could help myself by reaching out, loaded, angry, crying, I brought him up to my apartment. We clung together, fought each other, and in one glorious moment, found release. I fell asleep in his arms, not knowing his name, not caring, not even aware if I was to see him again. For one moment, I had been fully alive.

Arthur, that was his name, the big brooding man on the bus, who had a penchant for wearing Regina's perfume and stealing her paychecks. Regina knelt at the feet of this restless merchant sailor, his cock in her mouth, while clouds of Channel No. 5 toilet water wafted over her head. Every once in a while his fury erupted, and Regina was left lying in her own blood and teeth.

Run, Regina, run.

December 29, 1969. I'm drunk. I'm listening to the hilarious news on television. More draftees, more killings, more injustice. I can't hold on much longer. Is it my own unhappiness? I am not as holy as I wish to think. I hate the man I love. I hate myself for loving him. I hate his values, his estimation of who you are, how good your credit is, how much money you have. I have no money, no position. I live week by week, paycheck by paycheck, hate my work, hate what keeps me alive. I could have gone on if I was able to give and receive love. So, you say, what the hell do you want? So I didn't get it. So I didn't deserve it. So I didn't play the game. So they didn't play my game. Only fucking, literally and figuratively, is the whole game. Do it well and you will be a success. Do it with your heart and call it love and you can be sure you will get a good fucking-over. I am sick of my body demanding the touch of love, sick to my soul of all the ugliness.

Come on Youth, fight with all your weapons. Save this world for yourselves. We have only garbage. I am past it. Dump us, burn us, but don't become one of us. Be humble to your own. Give yourselves love; we won't recognize it.

If I could dream again, what would I dream?
I would dream that this was no dream,
that I was really loved.

The bus awaits, the program is bought, away we go to glory or to doom. We are where the action is, the comradeship, the sympathetic ear, the boast of winning the day before.

We look at each other, almost lovingly.

The ocean still sweeps those shores of memory, of desire. I skip beyond the waves, carrying my mother's drunkenly scrawled words beyond their reach. Her words, my words, her desire, my desire, her body, my body–only water and sand. But while I live and you read my words, we have built a dike against the blurring of time.

> *Try to understand and put up with me for a little while, so that you in your turn will never feel that you never knew me at all. That, I think, is the worst thing that could happen to a human being, to die and not have anyone know that you have lived.*

Rest, Regina, rest.

June 2, 1968
I plucked the leaf from the bough,
the crisp, firm leaf lay firmly in my palm.
It had a velvet touch, but the edges scratched my skin.
I should have understood the way then.
I walked barefoot on good solid earth
and felt the strength imported to my limbs.
My feet carried me here and there, and not seeing where I
went, I sank into a quagmire.
There my feet were useless, my legs, my arms, my mind sank
into sand.
In many walks throughout my life, I touched the mire
but still I walk
and seek the leaf.

Poetry, Regina, poetry. You loved your words most of all. They held you, Regina. On the bus, on the run, on the make. Words, Regina, words.

II.
The Politics of Thinking

The Politics of Thinking

Ideas have been both the prison and the hope of queer people, and I have lived in both. In the mid-fifties, my mother took me to a doctor because she thought something was not right with me. Perhaps it was the never-ending late-night telephone calls to Sheila, my fifteen-year-old co-worker in the five and dime. "Yes," said the doctor, his bookcase full of popular psychology books, "your daughter suffers from excess facial hair, definitely a sign of a hormonal imbalance." I thought it was because I was Jewish. Later in the decade, after having found me in bed with a young woman, my mother ran to another doctor, this time a psychiatrist. "My daughter is a lesbian!" my mother cried. "Don't say that," hushed the well-educated doctor, "that is like saying she has cancer."

For so long, we existed in their ideas about us, and that translated into judgment, enforced treatments, and often terror, shame, and despair. Now, gloriously, we have given ourselves an understanding of ourselves. We can trace our movement through time and economic systems, through systems of power and desire, through shifting definitions and connected communities. We now have sex and discourse, and often one is as exciting as the other. Our thinkers have given us room to breathe, creating a new paradigm for questioning the "natural." With all their play and all our seriousness, the vision of our own humanity, and therefore of all, only grows wider and deeper.

I am stunned when I think of the road I have traveled in the last forty years: from a pervert, policed and contained, to a queer lesbian fem woman who writes of sex and history. Decade by decade we suffered and fought our way to sense. This journey was made possible by lovers–lovers of the body and the mind. I have often thanked those who touched my breasts and spread my thighs, but now at the end of this century, I am honored by the touch of another kind of lover–the thinkers who tell me that perhaps it didn't have to be that way at all, perhaps we can understand things differently. These words are as exciting and as necessary as kisses.

One of the greatest joys of going to college in the 1950s was the discovery that ideas did not have to wear the same gray hopelessness as so much else of my working-class childhood. In college I sat in worn classrooms and ate at a rich man's table.

I was introduced to ideas that seemed in their own time large enough and complex enough to carry truth forever, and I learned that every generation had to let go of certainty as economics changed people and people changed their society and technology changed people's lives and poets changed their dreams. Here in this cauldron of youth, politics, and ideas, I left behind my Bronx and Bayside territories of loss and peered into the minds of other centuries to see where I could live.

I was most drawn to the intellectual drama of the Victorians; under the guidance of Dr. Viljoen, an elderly, frazzled woman whose lips were blurred with shaky red and whose cigarette never stopped glowing, I read the essays of Darwin and Huxley, of Arnold and Ruskin. Here I heard for the first time the cries of anguish that signal the most dire challenge to intellectual certainty. The Bible or Darwin, the past or the future, total commitment to what we know to be truth or the despair of waiting on a moonlit beach listening to the ceaseless pull of the tides that promise nothing we can be sure of–these were dramas of the mind that moved my heart. I know a little better now why I, as a Jew from the Bronx, a young fem woman opening up to lesbian love for the first time in her life, was drawn into these mid-nineteenth-century conflicts of faith and science, of the tension between grueling work and the need for daily beauty. Here was a time when power, and all the ideas that carried it, could be seen to be fallible, and in the cracks of certainty, I saw a place for myself. I also saw integrity and despair, not about money or love, but issuing from a concern about our fragility in the face of knowledge so huge we were afraid we would disappear.

Through my education, I began to understand that even though I was not of the ruling class, I could carry away ideas and make them mine. And so I did. Existentialism, with its resounding right to say no, with its brave loneliness, found a home in me. Marxism, with its call to pay attention to who eats and who does not, found a home in me. The ideas of Frantz Fanon and Albert Memmi, their understanding of colonized selves, of how much is lost in the psychological turmoil of cultural displacement, became like flesh to me. I still remember that late-fifties' afternoon when my Shakespeare professor drew the interlocking circles of the Great Chain of Being on the sun-drenched blackboard. I was charmed by this Elizabethan diagram of thought that suggested that people, at their best, could partake of the godhead and animals, in the full complexity of their development, could reach for the human sphere. Forty years later, these ideas still live in me, a gift given to me by teachers who could have no clue about what I would do with them in my life, a gift of ideas that allowed me to be an autonomous being no matter what social role others may have planned for a young woman like me.

Having ideas that differed from what the country was supposed to be thinking was not a popular stance in the late 1950s. I learned soon enough that the word *subversive* stood for the policing of thinking, whether that thinking led to action or not. In this decade I saw the power of ideas to both ruin lives and inspire courage of the highest kind. I listened carefully to the statements read against the banging of McCarthy's gravel as the House Un-American Activities Committee made victims out of defiant thinkers. "You will be held in contempt, sir," a committee man would say, as people like Paul Robeson struggled to explain their beliefs.

I was no longer a student by the time the black and women's movements poured their passions into the intellectual insurrections of the 1960s. But I was a teacher of students who needed these ideas, and I too was changed by them. Soon it became clear to me that rethinking American history the way Frederick Douglass had suggested in 1845, from the bottom up, was essential not just for those who lived the history of marginality but for all world thinkers. How could we have ever turned away from the ideas that led us to listen to those who create the wealth of nations? How could we ever have pretended that entrenched gender and racial power does not shape nations? We did for hundreds of years, until people rose up with their thinking and, unfazed by scorn and trivialization, changed once again the mix of ideas, changed once again the nature of hope.

Now I am fifty-eight years old, and I have retired from teaching, but because of my wonderful, international world of smart women friends and my work with the Lesbian Herstory Archives, I stand once again engaged with ideas, and my blood runs as hot. Now I sit with comrades and read Michel Foucault and Judith Butler, just as I read T. S. Eliot and James Joyce so many years ago. Now, as I did then–when I struggled to learn Eliot's world of high Protestant symbolism, translating some of his images into the walking dead of my mother's garment industry world, and just as I traveled with Stephen through a Catholic boyhood, until I found the moans of Molly in the closing pages of *Ulysses*–I experience the generosity of ideas, how they make me a citizen of the world.

And now I add the hope of postmodern thinking to my intellectual geology. What follows is my eclectic understanding of what is important in this current offering of ideas. I have not sat in a classroom speaking postmodernism; I have not read the French poststructuralist thinkers, male or female, and I do not have a job dependent on how well I manipulate the markers of its language in my latest book or article. But I have read *Queer Theory: An Introduction* by Annamarie Jagose, and to her I owe the outline of my thinking.

First there is the question of subjectivity–the process of becoming a self that is always re-forming in response to the forces of the world around it. Yes, I know this. To be working class is to experience the need to re-create one's self almost continuously if one wants to move about in the world of places and ideas, so the concept of "contested sites" or the idea of a mythical self that we use as if it were real is old hat in some ways. But I also know when to give respect to speakers who need to be all themselves in one self, those whose struggle to live is too severe to be undercut by theories of the nonexistent subject.

Then there is the deconstruction of what have passed for centuries as theories of knowledge, of philosophical regimes, of forced totalities, the myths of cohesion, the faith in foundationalism. I find nothing hopeless in this worldview of continuous disunities, in this belief that identities are created over and over again under the pressure of shifting social, historical, and linguistic terrain, in this questioning of the efficacy of one story for all. The commitment to engagement now exists not under a banner of absolutes–perhaps it exists under no banner at all (except when conservative forces say we cannot carry one)–but in the name of the complexity of the human experience.

I find no nihilism here, nor a cynical disavowal of the preciousness of human life. In my postmodern soul, I see a chance for a multiplicity of heard histories. I see the hope of power revealed and beauties created every day. My Marxism, my understanding that people must have enough to eat and a place to live and cures for their physical suffering and roses for the soaring of their dreams, becomes a more inclusive demand when it is coupled with the understandings of postmodern humility.

I do find some problems, however, with the present debates over this new presentation of very old uncertainties.

Postmodern thinking, with its richness of shifting perspectives, must never be just the plaything of academics; political struggle, in the face of economic injustice and social exclusion, must never be dismissed as meaningless behavior. All economic classes of students must have access to both the play and the power of these ideas. Two public events that I recently attended made me realize that there is a growing politics of thinking in this country, a politics and an economics of who will have the ability to explore unsettling ideas and new world images, the way I did as that unsophisticated student so many years ago.

The first site of disturbance was at a publicly funded college in New Paltz, New York, in November 1997. When women gathered to discuss sex in a conference sponsored by the Women's Studies Department, conservative forces called for the dismissal of the college's president and for the protection of "children" from such disturbing ideas. "It is an outrage that public money is used to fund such gatherings," said the governor of New York. SUNY, New Paltz, is home to a predominantly working- and lower-middle-class community of students. Representatives of the governor's office and members of the board of trustees met for long hours behind closed doors to determine what these students had a right to hear.

Two months later, I attended a discussion at Columbia University entitled "Intolerance and Sexuality." I expected a lively debate. Set in one of Columbia's on-campus theaters, the discussion was quiet and unfocused. The audience of mostly older people filed in quietly; the novelist Mary Gordon introduced the speakers as they entered, one after the other, and sat themselves down in a theatrically relaxed way. "I don't know why I am here," said one author, a gay man. "I haven't found anything to complain about." Except for the older straight literary figure who wanted to bring back a concept of sin that would include abortion, promiscuity, and sodomy, no one in the semicircle felt they had anything pressing to say about the topic. And then the gay author remembered that Maine had that very day voted to repeal its gay rights protection bill, but even this did not arouse him or the others out of their lethargy. Boredom predominated, and each speaker was greeted with polite applause from the audience.

All this decorum broke apart when it was time for questions from the audience. One woman, a visitor to the campus who had been to the SUNY conference, spoke in anger. "How can you all sit there in the comfort of this well-appointed space and act as if speaking about sexuality on a college campus is the norm?" She informed them about what had happened at New Paltz, an event that had made all the city's newspapers, and students' voices rang out through the theater. "They tried to fire the president!" one shouted. "The students organized and petitioned for their right to hear discussions about all kinds of sexual communities–why don't you address this?" another demanded. The few students in the audience began to walk out.

Then Mary Gordon came to life. "Yes, my husband teaches at New Paltz, and he says the campus is still traumatized by what happened." She spoke, half-turned in her chair, finally looking at the audience, like a person slowly waking up. But the evening was over. I left, bewildered like the others at the contrast between these two events.

Now I know what I was seeing: the politics of thinking. Privately funded schools can put on all the "literary" events they want; the accusation of the misuse of taxpayers' money is not going to be used like a club to stamp out discussions there. It is working-class schools that are going to be "protected" from the new ideas, the very ideas that these students need the most, the ideas for which I hope they will create a language not bogged down in impenetrable self-conscious prose. Postmodern discussion can be all the rage in Harvard and Yale, at Brown and Duke, but at public colleges, conservative forces are using the same techniques that have won them control of community school boards to police the campuses of higher learning.

When we add to this agenda the assault on affirmative action, the campaign to keep remedial help from working-class students in four-year public colleges, and the general downsizing of quality public college education, the picture becomes even clearer. Give postmodernism back to the young people; they have already found a suitable language to discuss it in–body piercing, music, performance, genderbending, their visions of the future.

But we who have been part of history longer have work to do to honor their explorations. In the newspaper on the day I was drafting this essay, an article appeared about a leader of a Christian family values organization who is leaving his not-for-profit organization to put his efforts into "jump-starting" a religious right third party whose agenda will be the elimination of abortion, homosexuality, and promiscuity. Fundamentalism has made queer people the enemy once again; while we delight in discussions of the performance of sex and gender, philosophers like John M. Finnis use the ancient decree of natural law and gay people's exclusion from it to carry us back into a time when we were Satan's spawn.

Here is a fragile union of crucial importance, whose challenge is to keep alive the generous textual insights of Eve Sedgwick, the dialectical and humane understandings of John D'Emilio, Liz Kennedy, and Jonathan Katz, to take pleasure in the clarity and power of Gayle Rubin as she dissects this society's (including our own) fear of sexual minorities, to keep dancing on the edge of definitions and questioned reality with Judith Butler, to learn from the hot and wise narratives of Pat Califia while we struggle to stop the advance of an iron-bound war machine with a fixed morality and a growing political army that has made us the people chosen for annihilation. Playing my part in this struggle to keep the intellectual roads open is the best way I know to honor that young woman who worked as a sales clerk by night and traveled through the world's thoughts by day.

Narratives of Liberation: Pluralities of Hope

A Syllabus for Sickos
– The measured words of Roger Kimball, editor of the *New Criterion*, published in the *Wall Street Journal*, November 5, 1997

In the presence of [us], Wing Biddlebaum, who for twenty years had been the town mystery, lost something of his timidity, and his shadowy personality, submerged in a sea of doubts, came forth to look at the world.
– Sherwood Anderson, in *Winesburg, Ohio*

As is true for many lesbian and gay people, my college years were also my coming-out years. In the 1950s, my only moments of erotic and emotional freedom were in shadowy places, places haunted by police and vice squads, flashing red lights and swirling nightsticks. I found wonders of community and touch in these places, but I also learned the scorching limitations of social exile.

In 1958, I entered Queens College, a then-free component of the City University system of New York and the campus where I was later to teach for nearly thirty years. Here, I and other working-class "queers," as we called ourselves then, met at a small table in the cafeteria, bolstering our fragile self-images with insider's gossip about the gay or lesbian author we had just read in English class. Surrounded by homophobic students and teachers, by cultural references to faggots and bull dykes, by the McCarthy-fueled hatred of subversives, we worked very hard to convince ourselves that we were not the grotesques of our campus world. We never thought then that we had the right to ask the university to care about us, our minds, our imaginations, our lives.

Some of us found a home in other struggles for social change that were finding a voice on the campuses. We knew that while we could not tell our fellow demonstrators where we spent our Friday and Saturday nights, we could draw hope and strength from the battles against nuclear arms, against the House Un-American Activities Committee, against the Vietnam War, and against segregation. Every mile on every march, every hour spent at endless meetings, every endured taunt and thrown bottle, every arrest carried an embedded hope that when we changed this society, there would be a place for queers. Then as now, college campuses were both a place of exile and a refuge.

By the end of the 1960s, the gay liberation movement had found its own feet alongside the civil rights and women's movements, changing the social expectations of this country. People were on the move, shaping history with their bodies, and I moved with them. First in 1970, when I joined the Gay Activist Alliance, a rowdy gathering of queers that met weekly in an abandoned firehouse on Wooster street in New York City to plan zaps against homophobic institutions and individuals. Then in 1973, when I was part of a group of gay men and women who formed the Gay Academic Union. Our goals were to challenge the homophobia and sexism that flourished on college campuses, to end the isolation of gay and lesbian students and teachers, to share our research and writing, and to inspire curriculum changes that would reflect the contributions of gays and lesbians to our culture. We met for two years, held conferences, published monographs, helped launch other chapters, and supported one another in our research and writing. I remember the 1973 conference for two reasons: it was the first conference of gay academic people "in the history of civilization" as Richard Gustafson asserted in his welcoming remarks, and we had to empty the hall in the midst of an impassioned speech by Edgar Z. Friedenberg, a renowned writer on education in America and Canada, because a bomb threat had been phoned in to the police. There we stood, out in the cold November night, half pleased that a meeting of two hundred gay academics could cause such a disturbance. It was at these early gatherings that I met Jonathan Katz, Julia Penelope Stanley, Martin Duberman, Gayle Rubin, and Deborah Edel—writers and activists who played a major role in shaping the next twenty years of lesbian and gay culture.

Also in 1973, the Lesbian Herstory Archives was born, and for twenty wonderful and exhausting years it occupied my apartment. Now I realize the archives were necessary because of what was *not* happening on college campuses: the stories that were not being told, the histories that were not being chronicled, the connections that were not being made, the richness of thought that was not being encouraged. In those days, I walked through my apartment late at night, gazing in wonder at the plentitude of lesbian cultural work, at the photographs of vibrant women from the forties, the boxes and boxes of letters and diaries, books, films, photographs, and special collections, struck by the paradox of the external cultural silence that surrounded us and this fullness of a community's self-expression. I knew we were not the first community to challenge enforced amnesia. Fifty years earlier a young man, Arthur Schomberg, had begun collecting every document of Caribbean and African American culture he could find after a teacher said to him that blacks had no history. Thus, the Schomberg Center for Research in Black Culture was born, a center that now enriches the world's scholarship. I remember the first time a college class came to tour the Lesbian Herstory Archives in the fall of 1980 as a visit of special meaning. The students were amazed at the vastness of materials pouring out over each other in a private home; they wanted to hear about the passion that could create such a collection, and they were angry at what had been kept from them.

In 1966, I went back to Queens College as a teacher of writing in the SEEK Program, an educational opportunity program born out of the social anger of young Black and Puerto Rican women and men who believed higher education had turned its back on them. For the next twenty-nine years, I was to be educated by these "nontraditional" students in the courage of the heart and mind when confronted with what academics now call "the hegemonic power of the colonizer." I have read hundreds of memoirs written by students depicting flights from countries that were no longer safe, describing their battle with a language that represents to them the loneliness of exile, and expressing their need for hope. It was these students, hundreds of thousands of them, who changed the face of American education, who gave back to our educational institutions a hope for all of us–the hope that the story of human culture would for the first time reflect the complexity and richness of all our differences, of all our narratives of liberation.

As honored as I was to teach the English Department's first official gay and lesbian literature course in 1993 and to co-teach a similar course at the CUNY graduate center the following year, I have long realized that I learned my deepest lessons about education and social change from the resistance and insistence of my SEEK students. What I learned was that the finest writing and thinking can happen only when there is hope in the mind and heart of the student, hope that her life is of some importance, that her ideas will be honored with a hearing, that her choice of language will be respected with a response, that the risks she takes will be valued. Some students can take this minimal academic encouragement for granted, but the students I worked with for all these years could not. Many of them had neither the skin color nor the accent nor the money to qualify for being heard. A gay and lesbian struggle for academic inclusion and respect is part of this larger discussion: How do we create the possibilities of hope embodied in narratives of liberation, narratives that are, according to Patrick Taylor, a Caribbean social thinker, "the stories of lived freedom, the stories of individuals and groups pushing up from below to reveal the ambiguity and multilayeredness of reality" (Taylor, 15)?

The movement that started in 1973 both in the academy and in grassroots community projects transformed the cultural and social possibilities for queer people. The courage of gay and lesbian students to ask for what they needed was backed by the courage of lesbian and gay teachers to risk their jobs by responding with gay inclusion in the curriculum. Our cultural workers, the writers, theorists, historians, philosophers, and political and social thinkers, created new texts, revisioned old ones, and ended the conspiracy of silence surrounding the nature of the desire that had cloaked so many of the canon's classic authors. Lesbian and gay archives, specialized collections, bibliographic guides, study centers all now stand behind the student who proposes a queer exploration. No longer can a senior professor douse a student's enthusiasm with the words "It sounds interesting, but I doubt you will find enough information to complete your project."

The bookshelves are overflowing with our texts; the language of our inquiry has spilled over both into popular culture and into the ivory towers of think tanks and exclusive universities. We are a hot cultural item, with major university presses jockeying for their lesbian and gay multivolume series and major publishers trying to cast their net over the more sellable authors. In short, we have become a community from whom money can be made, but we must continue to be an intellectual community from whom changes can be expected, changes in how gender is thought about, how power is conceptualized, how desire becomes resistance. Publishers have their reasons for calling for our manuscripts, but we must have our reasons for creating them. We must ask ourselves as we pursue our demands for inclusion in the places that still turn away from our cultural richness, What are the stories we want to tell? What narratives are we piecing together from communal pain and strength, from professional and personal excellence of thought and imagination, and how do they join with the stories of others who are fighting for the right to tell their stories in their own words from the fullness of their own histories?

Almost every discipline included in a contemporary college catalogue has been touched by the new interpretations, the new information provided by the gay cultural workers of the last twenty years. Anthropology's beginnings must be seen in a different light. The patriarchal figure of Franz Boas, birthing the new science in his wood-lined Columbia university study, must now confront the mothers of anthropology; the bisexual Margaret Mead, who insisted that sexual development in differing cultural settings suggested that desire was a constructed value, long before we had heard a French word on the topic; the lesbian Ruth Benedict, who transformed thinking about culture with her plea for a multicultural understanding of difference; and the free-spirited Zora Neale Hurston, who found a way to use the skills of anthropology to commemorate a people rather than to objectify them. Surely students have a right to ponder the connections among gender, sexual desire, and race, as well as the production of original thinking that the lives of these three women represent.

Think of the missed teaching opportunity in computer courses if the paradox of Alan Turning's life is not discussed with the students—how he was forced to lead an encoded life while he imagined a machine that would break codes. Think of the opportunity an educator has to give technology a human face, to place its creation and use back in the narrative of the human need for touch.

The work of Liz Kennedy and Madeline Davis in their sociological and historical study of a Buffalo working-class lesbian bar community, *Boots of Leather, Slippers of Gold: The History of a Lesbian Community,* has ensured that sweeping descriptions of any decade not be trusted. Thanks to historians like them, stultifying national norms are routinely subverted by communities of outsiders, and queer history is tense with contradictions, rich with examples of communal refusal of predetermined historical categories. Because of the work of gay and lesbian historians, every historical period is being reexamined for its other histories, the underbellies of the known stories. Students embarking on the journeys of their own lives should be given the gift of complex knowledge, the insight and encouragement to find the text not spoken, to piece together the bones of hidden histories so they may more fully live their own.

Perhaps it is the study of literature that has been most liberated by the ending of silences and the emergence of multiple readings. Years of misrepresentation have been swept away by the possibility of open discussion of the roles of gender, sexuality, and passion in the formation of a text. More and more biographies are giving us fuller portraits for understanding the relationship between desire and creation. "Not until 1952, when she set up a stable and happy life in the household of Lota de Macedo Soares, could Elizabeth Bishop take objective account and make direct artistic use of her difficult childhood" (Millier, 1). When Mary Renault writes in a 1966 letter, "All through those years my inner personae occupied two sexes, too indiscriminately to take part in a sex war" (Sweetman, 252), she helps us understand one of the sources of the vitality of her Greek homoerotic fictional world.

And when Lillian Smith sadly writes about her inability to be open about her forty-year love affair with Paula Snelling, she throws her other work, the documenting of the spiritual bankruptcy of southern racism, into stark relief. She was, she says, held back in her honesty about her life by her shame, "my shame about something different and completely good. It has been that shame that has destroyed the keen edge of a pattern of love that was creative and good" (Gladney, 136).

Emily Dickinson, Amy Lowell, Willa Cather, Sara Orne Jewett, Sara Teasdale, H. D., Elizabeth Bishop, Nella Larsen, May Swenson, Muriel Rukeyser, Audre Lorde, Adrienne Rich, Mary Oliver all have markings in their work of the imaginative complexity of same-sex desire and their innovative struggles with the confines of gender. Their choice of language, of images, of vision, the very formation of their texts, like those of Shakespeare, Herman Melville, Henry James, Walt Whitman, Countee Cullen, James Baldwin, Federico Garcia Lorca, Langston Hughes, Allen Ginsberg, and Richard Howard, challenge us to new readings of how desire is encoded or announced in a text, how this private discourse affects the public themes of the work, allowing us to get glimpses of how the hope of self-disclosure, or the fear of it, lives deep in the mystery of literary language and structure. With these insights, students have the chance to read all the stories a text can tell, without shame, without restrictions.

Our narratives of liberation begin with a touch, begin with the body asking for a pleasure that has no social place; out of this quiet moment, a cultural transformation takes place. With this touch come the questions–about the permanence of gender, the cultural power of desire, the relationship between parody and what we think is real.

In America today–or perhaps I should say in the world today–these are dangerous questions to be asking. When we join them to the inquiries of feminism, of postcolonialism, of economic determinism, we can see that a huge moment of questioning is at hand. Narratives of liberation "lift human agents out of their closed realms to bring them into universal history, insisting on the fundamental unity, even in diversity, of all humanity" (Taylor, 22). Any social system or ideology that attempts to deny or negate this human possibility is a destroyer of human hope.

Gay and lesbian studies and the "frivolities of deconstruction" have become the symbol of the loss of America to uncivilized and ungendered masses. When Harold Bloom agonizes over the loss of the traditional canon (an interesting phrase), when authors make millions of dollars proving how illiterate some Americans are because they do not know what others have decided is the correct sum of our cultural knowledge, when theories of the biological inferiority of whole groups of people again make front-page news, when educators announce that reform schools are the only answer to hopelessness, when fundamentalism calls for the killing of difference in the protection of sacred truth, then we have some sense of the power of our new readings and of the terror of destabilization they inspire. Of all the reasons I can name why gay and lesbian studies should be part of the college curriculum across disciplines–because it would be intellectually honest and conceptually challenging, because it would serve to demarginalize the lives of a good number of the students we are paid to teach, because the resources now exist to do this easily and interestingly, because it would make for more lively and involving classroom discussions and writing, because it would give the academy a chance to involve communities of activists and cultural workers from beyond the limited world of the campus–there is one reason that stands out as the most compelling.

People are moving all around this globe in unprecedented numbers–following jobs, fleeing catastrophes, finding new air to breathe. There is a great intermingling of ideas, religions, languages, desires. Some are comfortable with this multitude of choices; others are rushing to shore up the boundaries of the known world by reasserting a politics of exclusion and deprivation. When all else fails, they reach for guns. Teachers and students will not be able to hide from this tension. Gay and lesbian studies are often dismissed as being trivial, faddish, a hocus-pocus of language and an inconsequential expression of attitude: read our books, listen to our poets, touch your lover. Think of shame and self-disclosure, of ostracism and communal creation, of difference and coalitions, of hatred and beauty, of exile and love, of conformity and independent thought, of performance and wit, of the body and all its ideas. This is what gay and lesbian studies can offer.

Gay and lesbian people are not alone in wanting the hope of a new narrative of education; now is the time to form alliances among the communities who see the importance of bringing Wing Biddelbaum out of the shadows, draped in the mysteries of his suppressed story. This shadowy figure will appear differently in different histories; the stories he brings to the surface will be spoken in many tongues; he may be a woman or a man or both in the same body–but this emergence, while sometimes frightening because it is unexpected and uncontrolled, will call to us to find common ground on which to protect the dignity of difference and the possibility of hope.

Bibliography

Anderson, Sherwood. "Hands" in *Winesburg, Ohio.* New York: Viking Press, 1958.

Gay Academic Union. *The Universities and the Gay Experience: Proceedings of the Conference Sponsored by the Women and Men of the Gay Academic Union.* November 23 and 24, 1973. New York: Publications Committee. Gay Academic Union, 1974.

Gladney, M. R., ed. *How Am I to Be Heard? Letters of Lillian Smith.* Chapel Hill: University of North Carolina Press, 1993.

Millier, Brett C. *Elizabeth Bishop: Life and the Memory of It.* Berkeley: University of California Press, 1993.

Sweetman, David. *Mary Renault: A Biography.* New York: Harcourt Brace, 1993.

Taylor, Patrick. *The Narrative of Liberation: Perspectives on Afro-Caribbean Literature, Popular Culture, and Politics.* Ithaca, NY: Cornell University Press, 1989.

On Rereading
"Esther's Story"

I turned to touch her, but she took my hand away from her breast. "Be a good girl," she said....The words, the language of my people, floated through my head–untouchable, stone butch....

Whenever I am applauded for having given over so much of my personal living space to house the Lesbian Herstory Archives in the first twenty years of its life, I answer quite truthfully that the archives has given me more than I ever gave it. In periods of illness, it provided endless small tasks that kept me stimulated and productive; the constant stream of materials kept me current in a complex cultural discussion; and I found long-lasting friends among the many women who came to my home on a search for information or for self. One of the results of this constant interplay between my private life and a river of news and personalities was that I became comfortable with shifting perspectives;

in fact, it almost seemed a given that whenever I was sure I knew the only answer to something, someone or some text would force me to rethink or to pull back from a sweeping generalization to arrive at a very specific particular. I thought I would lose all these gifts when the archives, like a daughter come of age, moved from my home to its own. But I was wrong.

In its four-year life in the Park Slope section of Brooklyn, the archives has made new friends, two of whom are Chelsea Elisabeth Goodwin and her lover, Rusty Mae Moore, both transgendered women. I had spoken to Chelsea several times on the phone about transgender issues and she had sent me copies of several position papers she had written on the transgender struggle for civil rights recognition. I knew that Chelsea had been volunteering at the archives for some months, but I had not yet met her. Then one day, when I was giving a tour of the archives, I led my small group up to the second floor, where all the mail is processed. There, bending over the long table filled with newly arrived newsletters, was a very tall, very thin butch woman who turned to greet us. "Hi, I'm Chelsea," she said with a quick turn of her head.

"Finally, we meet," I said, both curious and moved, as I often am when I see a new volunteer giving up her time to do the often tedious work the archives demands. As far as I knew, Chelsea was the first transgendered woman to work with the archives, and I knew she must have felt some trepidation about how she would be welcomed. The archives collective is made up of approximately twenty women who see the world from very different perspectives. While I knew there had been an ongoing discussion about how to define the word *woman*, the collective had sorted itself out and Chelsea's help was greatly appreciated. Before continuing my tour, I thanked her for the material she had sent me and promised we would talk later. We did meet several times more after this first encounter–at speaking events and at archives open houses. More and more, Chelsea revealed herself to be a courtly and caring lover of women. At one archives event, she made a stirring speech about how older fem women such as her lover, Rusty, had brought great beauty into her life. At the close of that evening, she took leave of me by kissing the back of my hand. But still I did not know Chelsea, other than by the complexity of her choices: to be a woman, to love another transgendered woman, to identify herself as butch.

Our relationship deepened one hot summer day in the basement of the new archives. I joined Chelsea at the processing table, and together we waded through the never-ending stacks of periodicals. While we worked, we spoke about sex, about butch-fem relationships, and about the difficulties of organizing a marginalized group. Chelsea spoke as a committed activist who was struggling to keep the transgendered-transsexual movement dynamic and inclusive. She told me about her younger days as a street transsexual, when she was schooled in survival by Sylvia Rivera, the sweet, tough queen whose young face had been photographed in front of the Stonewall bar the night of our insurrection in 1969. Left behind by the mainstream respectable gay liberation movement, Sylvia now lived with Chelsea and Rusty in their collective trans home around the corner from the archives.

The light from the naked bulb under which we worked flashed over Chelsea's face, a strong, chiseled face, with thin arching eyebrows and a prominent, bony nose. As she spoke of her days on the street, when she was always running from the police, and her constant search for a place to spend the night, all the years in between those gritty times and the present seemed to melt away. I listened not only to her words but to the turn of her head, the softness of her demeanor, the passion of her vision. Here I was in my late fifties, witnessing once again the power of memory to inform conviction, the conviction of one's right to survive. Still haunted by the realities of street life, Chelsea had asked not to be left alone at the archives in case the police showed up, as they sometimes did when some door or window left open triggered our building alarm. Chelsea's words poured into the steamy basement, demanding that room be made for another layer of lesbian history.

Before the heat drove us upstairs, I responded to Chelsea's concerns about how best to serve a growing movement for liberation with memories of some of my own struggles with the early spokeswomen of the lesbian-feminist movement, my anger at their disdain for the bar community that had given me my first lessons in queer defiance, my fears about the exclusions deemed necessary when a political passion calls for a united front. Feeling like a veteran of a half-won war, I urged Chelsea to learn from our mistakes as well as from our victories. "You have a chance to do things differently," I remember saying. Behind those words was my conviction that if we had done things differently as lesbian-feminist women, as a gay liberation movement in the thirty years since Stonewall, Chelsea and her comrades would not have to be fighting for their most basic rights in the 1990s. But we had been so sure then that we knew who was a "woman" and who a "man," what gender meant and what it did not, what embarrassed us and what made us feel, in our own peculiar way, at home. It is one of the complex ironies of liberation movements that often the passion of their certainties creates the need for future, more inclusive visions of emancipation.

My final words to Chelsea that afternoon were to urge her to call me if I could ever be of any help to her.

In August of that summer, 1997, Chelsea took me up on my vague offer. She reminded me of the group she and Rusty had organized, the Metropolitan Gender Network, and asked me to fill in for Leslie Feinberg, who was too ill to speak as scheduled on the following Sunday. My first response was to wonder what could I say to a transgendered group. What qualified me to appear before this forum? Chelsea listened to my fears and then patiently told me that my writings about butch-fem relationship had helped to open up the discussion of gender representation for many communities. What posed as political and cultural modesty on my part was really a lack of understanding of the transgendered, transfolk community and my fear of moving into their world. I was condescending both to my own work and to the members of the

Metropolitan Gender Network. But years of work with the archives had taught me that when I was frightened of a new forum, that was exactly the time when history would speak to me, both to my head and to my heart.

I spent the next few days thinking about what my text could be. I decided to look over my work in my first book, *A Restricted Country*, to see if I could find a passage that would be a good starting point for discussion. Like a preacher preparing for her Sunday sermon, I searched for my chapter and verse. I found what I was looking for in "Esther's Story," a story I wrote in the 1980s to pay homage to a passing woman whom I had met in the Sea Colony, a 1960s working-class lesbian bar in Greenwich Village. Like other pieces in this 1987 book, "Esther's Story" was written (and the events in it re-visioned) from both the perspective of my lesbian feminism and my need to push against lesbian-feminist boundaries of acceptable history. I was determined to keep alive the world of my bar community with its one-night stands and sexually diverse clientele. Esther was a woman in her forties who passed for a man. The story tells of my amazement at her tenderness and describes how her hands shook when she first held me and how my young woman's body reached out to her for more:

> *Through my blouse, I could feel her hands like butterflies shaking with respect and need. Younger lovers had been harder, more toughened to the joy of touch, but my passing woman trembled with her gentleness. I opened to her, wanting to wrap my fuller body around her leanness. She was pared down for battle, but in the privacy of our passion she was soft and careful. We kissed for a long time. I pressed my breasts hard into her, wanting her to know that even though I was young, I knew the strength of our need, that I was swollen with it.*

But when I reread the story keeping in mind what I had and had not allowed myself to say about Esther's sense of self and gender, I saw clearly (and indeed, I knew this at the time I wrote the story) that I was being simplistic in my description of Esther's desires. I was trying to serve two histories at once. I knew that if I had written "Esther wanted to be a man," the story would have been dismissed and so would Esther and all I wanted for her in the new world of the 1980s. This balancing act led me to cast Esther's "maleness" in a more womanly way. It was as if I were attempting to slide under a descending iron gate and carry all that was important with me to safety before it crashed to the ground.

> *She told me how she had left Ponce, Puerto Rico, her grown sons, and her merchant sailor husband, to come to America to live like she wanted....She enjoyed driving the taxi, and because her customers thought she was a man, they never bothered her. I looked at her, at the woman in a neat white shirt and gray pants, and wondered how her passengers could be so deceived. It was our womanness that rode with us in the car, that filled the night with tense possibilities.*

Now I must ask myself who was the deceived one. This forced questioning of what we need to be real or true or right holds for me the deepest importance of liberation movements. If I know the dreams of only my own, then I will never understand where my impulse for freedom impinges on another history, where my interpretation of someone's life is weakened by my own limits of language, imagination, or desire. Chelsea's invitation to speak to her group had made me revisit my own text and realize that even when I thought I had been preserving a life, I was perhaps burying it. Esther's story is not finished, and my own understanding of butch and fem, of the drama of gender, of what the mind wants to do with the body and what the body wants to tell the mind, of what societies will do to keep gender certainties in place and of how women will survive all that is both created for them and taken from them must be constantly challenged by new voices demanding attention.

For one moment the Lower East Side was transformed for me: unheard of elegance, a touch of silk had entered my life. Esther's final gift. We never shared another night together. Sometimes I would be walking to work and would hear the beeping of a horn. There would be Esther rounding the corner in her cab with her passenger who thought she was a man.

Lesbian Sex and Surveillance

*Decisions of individuals relating to homosexual con-
duct has been subject to state intervention throughout the history of Western civilization.*
– Chief Justice Burger in his concurring opinion in
Bowers v Hardwick, 1986

*Most female homos hangouts are on Third Street,
and here a few feet away from the women's prison,
in a small, smoky and raucous saloon every Friday
night is held a lesbian soiree at which young girls,
eager to become converts, meet the already initiated.
These parties are presided over by an old and dis-
gusting excuse for a woman, who is responsible for
inducing thousands of innocent girls to lead unnatural lives…. Homos are not molested by police if
they remain in the district and don't bother others
on the theory that you can't do away with them,
and as long as they're with us, it's better to segre-
gate them in one section where an eye can be kept
on them.*
– From *New York Confidential*, 1948

If you didn't have on three pieces of women's cloth-ing, honey, you rode. You had to have a bra, nylon drawers and girls socks; otherwise you were arrested for impersonating a man. I sewed lace on my socks so the cops wouldn't have any problems seeing they were women's socks.
–Riki Stryker, speaking of the bar raids of the 1950s

After engaging in lesbian history work for over twenty-five years, I have discovered that certain motifs haunt me. They change with the times, as do the cast of characters and the forms the cultural con-frontations take, but there are themes, even in this postmodern time, that remain. Or perhaps these are the tropes that have come to symbolize the wounds and victories of my own queer history. I am thinking now of my long experience with sexual surveillance.

I have the unique privilege of being one of the few people to have been a speaker at both the Barnard conference on feminism and sexuality in New York City in 1982 and the SUNY, New Paltz, conference on women's sexuality in 1997. At both these gatherings, sexual talk by women was under close scrutiny. At the earlier conference, the ones patrolling the discussion were other women; at the more recent gather-ing, representatives of Concerned Americans for a Moral Society were in attendance along with a SUNY member of the board of trustees and a rep-resentative from the New York governor's office. All these good people mobilized themselves when they received word that a public university was sponsoring a conference, under the aegis of the women's studies program, that included references to lesbianism, sex toys, and S/M sexuality.

It has taken almost twenty years for a family discussion to become a national one, for sisters to be replaced by gray-suited men and properly attired straight women, but the atmosphere created by these watchdogs was much the same: anxious organizers, late-night telephone calls warning speakers that the conference might be disrupted, pressure on the convening institution to cancel the event, a physical presence meant to intimidate, and far-reaching communal consequences.

Even though my chemo treatments had left me exhausted and I had warned Amy Kesselman, one of the organizers of the conference, that she should be prepared for my having to cancel, I knew on that rain-drenched morning I had to be in New Paltz. When Amy called me the week before, concern pouring into her voice, to warn me about the possibility of disruption and to tell me of the struggle she had waged to keep the college's administration open to the event, I felt my blood warm up. I knew these battles deep in my gut, and this surge of engagement was a good antidote to the poison in my veins.

From my first forays into the Greenwich Village bars of the 1950s, I had understood that to be queer meant to travel in policed territories. Confinement made us easy targets; bar raids and street violence were frequent companions, and often the police were the perpetrators, not the protectors. A set of rules was laid down for us, encouraging over the years a responding body of survival lore. Along with the cigarette smoke and beer fumes that clung to our clothes long after Saturday night went the warnings about what to wear and whom to touch. Even though I was a fem, I dressed carefully for my nights out. What kind of world am I entering, I would think, where the police are with us even in the privacy of our closets? My slacks, sometimes men's slacks, because they were cheaper and fitted more comfortably around my big-hipped body, could become a reason for a representative of the state to thrust his hand down my pants. The cut of one's clothes or the placement of buttons were cause for verbal harassment and worse. This threatened surveillance of our clothing did not stop us from "vining back," but it served as a reminder that even that which lay against our skin was subject to state control.

A great part of the excitement of the sixties, of the power of the liberation movements, was leaving this kind of surveillance behind. Of course, it was replaced by the cameras and note pads of the FBI agents who followed the peace parades and infiltrated SANE meetings, but some-how that was different. Political activity was open dissension; sexual activity and its surveillance were secrets within secrets. Shame was com-panion to my fear in the earlier decade, making the surveillance an act of punishment in itself, but when I marched with thousands of others to end the Vietnam War, the whole nation was watching. One thing the sixties taught me was that powerless people could take over the streets, could challenge mammoth institutional vehicles like the Pentagon or segrega-tion or the surveillance of a community. Every time the sixties is por-trayed as a drug haze, this knowledge is betrayed.

We know now that starting in the late 1950s, the FBI was keeping the DOB (Daughters of Bilitis) and Mattachine Society under close watch, that as we left the closet and the bars, their eyes followed us. In 1965, when a group of gay men and lesbians held a gala costume ball to raise money for the Council on Religion and the Homosexual, the San Francisco police stood outside the doors, snapping photographs of every-one who entered and left. Oral histories tell of several lesbian teachers desperately trying to escape out of a back door so that they would not lose their jobs in the glare of a flash of light.

I remember one night in the early '70s when I had left the bars to attend the first dance held by the New York chapter of DOB in its new loft space. I took in the balloons hanging from the ceilings, the toned-down women in flannels and dungarees, and labeled it all innocuously tacky and boringly safe. They must be kidding, I thought, turning to leave, longing for the excitement of the sexually charged women of the Sea Colony–when all of a sudden, cops poured through the door, with the same look of disgust on their faces I had seen in the darkened streets outside the bars. However innocent I had found the DOB version of celebration, to the eyes of the state these women were just as deviant, just as needful of watching as my butch-fem bar comrades. But in the large, open space of the DOB gathering, with its wholesome decorations, the police invasion seemed ludicrous. I laughed at them that night. Their blundering antics could destroy the tenderness of touch in a darkened bar, but there was nothing for them to put their hands on in the clearly political air of the DOB gathering.

One of the joys of my work with the Lesbian Herstory Archives is compiling its documentation of the paranoia and historical contradictions of surveillance. In our subject file on the FBI and its relationship with the American lesbian community, we have copies of its surveillance records, won for us by the Freedom of Information Act: white sheets with blacked-out lines, but with enough visible to read about the government's vigilance–the names of the founders of DOB, the description of the women visiting the San Francisco office–enough peers out of the still-hidden records to allow one to see the government's concern about this embryonic movement of organized deviants. Last year, we received a special collection that tells the story of a lesbian who became a minor celebrity in the late 1950s when she went public with her story of her FBI-sponsored surveillance work of left-wing groups. In the context of the Lesbian Herstory Archives, the picture of this small, dark, very butch woman sitting at her typewriter as she informs on subversives forces us to let go of easy understandings of marginality. All archives, not just lesbian and gay ones, are sites of retextualization, where acts and words resurface in the glare of another cultural time; they are places where those abused by national power or societal ignorance can outlast the small minds and bitter hearts of their persecutors. The revelation of the Dartmouth letters of the 1930s protesting the presence of too many "Jew boys" on Dartmouth's campus, which were read at the opening ceremonies of the school's new Jewish Center, reflects how archival documents can exist in both an air of condemnation and one of hope. In the same manner, the Lesbian Herstory Archives is a place where records of public intimidation can be answered with stories of private resistance.

In the 1970s and '80s, while the FBI and the police were still observing and controlling the lives of sexually "deviant" women, another kind of surveillance surfaced. Swept up in the lesbian-feminist movement, I no longer feared the vice squad. Freed from this daily surveillance, some of us began to explore, in public words and deeds, the rich diversity of lesbian sexual desire. However, at the same time, the anti-violence-against-women struggle was undergoing a transformation, deepening its position that pornography was the basis of all acts of violence against women. Many of us had been active in the anti-violence campaigns of the early seventies, but it was clear that sexuality, and the perceived need to control it, was going to be a contested site in the 1980s. This was a discussion first and a "war" later, among feminist women, many of whom were the lesbian-feminist leaders of the cultural celebrations of the 1970s.

New texts of lesbian desire launched the conflict. In 1979, Pat Califia founded the lesbian-feminist S/M group Samois; in 1981, the *Heresies* collective published their sex issue, which included my essay on the courage of butch-fem sexual relationships in the 1950s, as well as "Feminism and Sadomasochism" by Pat Califia, "What We're Rollin Around in Bed With" by Cherrie Moraga and Amber Hollibaugh, and Paula Webster's "Pornography and Pleasure." To cap it all off, in the following year, Samois edited *Coming to Power*, an anthology of lesbian-feminist S/M writings. Now there were two streams of feminist discourse about women's sexuality, and they were to meet in a torrent of passion on both sides when Carole Vance and others organized a conference at Barnard College on April 24, 1982, entitled "The Scholar and the Feminist IX–Toward a Politics of Sexuality."

That afternoon was to mark my first experience with the painful role of being deemed a traitor by one's own allies. I had received calls the night before alerting me to the probability of a picket line against the conference, organized by Women Against Pornography, and giving me the even more stunning news that the college had decided to confiscate the booklet that served as the program of the day's events. One of the original booklets sits now at the archives, testifying to both the weakness of the sponsoring college and the silence of the feminist community about this most flagrant example of censorship.

Yes, there was a picket line that morning and leaflets were handed out declaring some of us "sex perverts" because of what we had publicly said about sexual desire and history. Yes, there were warnings that such discussions would not be tolerated. But even more frighteningly, a decade of internal surveillance was launched that day. I would receive calls asking me did I really say that on such and such a day; did I really stand behind the right of S/M women to practice their desire; was I writing about butch-fem in the past or present–for which there was really no correct answer, because neither was to be tolerated. It would be easy to dismiss all of this as a small sectarian skirmishes, except that federal forces of sexual control, like the Meese Commission on pornography, The Family Protection Act devotees, and the religious and political right now employed the language of anti-pornography feminism in public statements and proposed legislation. In 1986, the Supreme Court gave its highest opinion about a homosexual's right to private touch. The Bowers *v* Hardwick decision made the invasion of our bedrooms a legal right. Whether this country is policing the act or the individual, our bodies and our memories are marked by state control.

I had come a long way from the vice squad-haunted bars of the 1950s where our sexual practice, not our talk, was the target of the state's surveillance. In those days, we did not even conceive of public debates about "deviant" desire. By the end of the 1980s, Andrea Dworkin, Catharine MacKinnon, Julia Penelope, Robin Morgan, Sheila Jeffries lined up on one side of the issue, Gayle Rubin, Pat Califia, Carole Vance, Ann Snitow, Amber Hollibaugh, Dorothy Allison, and myself lined up on the other side. The sense of ideological surveillance moved from direct encounters to internalized voices to looking over one's shoulders to see who would be hunting down one's words. Some perfectionists felt it pushed back public work for many years. Others, like myself, found it gave us a reason to keep working, though never without doubt. Would my stories of asses and hands, cunts and dildos, history and need hurt lesbian women? I still ask that question.

In the early 1990s, with the growing strength of queer studies and the postmodern notion to doubt everything, the feminist feuds seemed to be reduced to a dated rehashing of old grievances. Here were new questions, new couplings of gender and sex, a new way to read. Names like Judith Butler and Eve Sedgwick attracted a great deal of attention. Transgendered writers and thinkers added a rich new source of experience and thinking about everything we had been struggling with for over twenty years. The wonderful richness of the dialectical method was at work again–synthesizing and, like a good composter, squeezing out the gold of fresh new ideas.

That is why it came as such a shock to be thrown back into the realization that women talking about sexuality in a place deemed public was still an unacceptable event in 1997. The event at SUNY, New Paltz, with its outpouring once again of the forces of surveillance, was a slap in the face, a forceful reminder that feminists and queers need to see and honor their connections. The queer theory celebrators who often hold prestigious jobs in private universities have to be concerned with the efforts that are going on in publicly funded colleges and universities to control the flow of ideas deemed subversive. Often it is the women, some in tenuous positions in their underfunded and underrespected women's studies departments, who bear the brunt of this surveillance. With the headiness of queer theory, I had come to think of women's studies as a rather old-fashioned pursuit, dusty with the niceties of the seventies. That morning in New Paltz showed me how wrong I was and how dangerously isolated both the students and the teachers in women's studies could become. I also saw that morning, as women carefully defended their right to talk about sex to the silent observers, that some of the chutzpah and theoretical independence of queer theory would be a powerful addition to the world of women's studies. That morning I saw how much we needed to honor our connected communities.

The moral indignation of Governor Pataki and the fury of Candace de Russy, a SUNY trustee; the call for the college president's resignation by the "moral" right; the outrage of some parents, who kept referring to their college-age sons and daughters as "children" who needed to be protected from such filth; and the 1950s' language of hatred employed by Roger Kimball (a "so-called educated man," as my working-class mother would have said) in his article for the *Wall Street Journal* entitled "A Syllabus for Sickos"–all these are powerful reminders to us of what awaits autonomous women talking about sex at the end of the twentieth-century.

When Larry Kramer in his *New York Times* Op-Ed piece announcing his disgust with the Sex Panic activists called on lesbians to speak out against the renewed possibility of gay men's public sexual pleasure, and the perils of sexual activity in general, he revealed his ignorance about this current battle and its long history. Lesbians are still fighting for the right to just talk about sex and culture without the surveillance of the state or of others who want to tell us what is "natural" for women. And those who would curtail our sexual discourse are growing larger and more powerful in many countries of the world. The increasing religious moral fervor in this country, the growing call for the blood of sexual offenders, the narrowing of allowable sexual tastes and discussions in the arts and in electronic communication are disturbing expressions of a national sexual panic, a phenomenon predicted by Gayle Rubin in her 1984 essay, "Thinking Sex: Notes for a Radical Theory of the Politics of Sexuality." The protection of women, children, the family, and the white Christian God from the contamination of sexual or racial or religious "deviants" is on its way to becoming national policy.*

Pataki's watchdogs could have had no idea all this was in my mind as I tried to give a brief history of lesbian sexuality that morning in New Paltz. My time of twenty minutes had shrunk to eight because of the long speeches the president and Amy had to make to explain why the conference had a right to exist. My fellow keynote speakers and I exchanged notes as we sat waiting for our time to speak. "This is like twenty years ago," Roz Petchesky scribbled to me. "We have to avoid their negative energy," whispered Eugenia Acuna. I looked out over the audience, above the heads of those who had come to keep their eyes on us, their moving hands writing down our policed words, to the over two hundred young people who had gathered to launch the day of sexual exploration. They have always been the hope, the reason it is so important not to let the silence fall.

Things are not really the same. I am at the end of my life, not the beginning. I am not afraid of disclosure and only rarely ashamed. The end of the century is not the same as the middle of it. I know now that the eyes of the watchers are cold stones even when the sun of their convictions is riding high in the political sky. I know now that surveillance is the weapon of the insecure, the frightened, the pinched. I still fear, however, the human act of policing thought and speech, of hands holding pens to take down our words, never allowing themselves to enter into the messy world of debate. I still fear those who enter rooms cloaked in silent power and, while we speak, plan their retaliations. Surveillance is not seeing; it is the quiet planning of prisons.

From a letter sent to the Lesbian Herstory Archives, November 1980:

I have been thinking a lot lately about my early days as a lesbian (I recently celebrated my 39th birthday and with it my 20th year as a dyke) and remembered something I thought you might find interesting....

I lived at home in 1960 (age 19). So did my lover. Sometimes we went to cheap hotels in the Times Square area, but often even this was hard to arrange. Somehow we heard of a woman on 14th Street who rented out rooms to lesbians (by the hour or the night I no longer remember) and despite our terror (we were after all, 2 *very* middle-class girls) of what we might find there, we went. The downstairs buzzer said Amazons Ltd. on it. We were greeted at the door by a smiling woman who took us into the kitchen, made us some tea and sat and talked with us for a while.

Then she left us alone. The kitchen was at one end of the long hallway off of which there were several rooms. I guess these were the rooms she rented out for we could sometimes hear muffled sounds coming from them. I don't remember ever actually seeing anyone else there. We never rented a room (still too afraid to acknowledge to someone else our erotic feelings) but we did go there frequently that cold winter to sit and talk with her in the kitchen or to be by ourselves in the parlor room at the other end of the hallway. The woman, whose name I wonder if I ever knew, never asked for money or pressured us in any way. It was, for us, a safe space and now I wonder about that woman and would certainly love to hear of anyone else who ever went there.

*The Clinton "sex scandal," which is unfolding as I revise this essay, raises interesting questions about the national stance on heterosexual private and public sexual mores. It is also clear that there are several cultural debates going on all at once that have as a subtext the role of women's sexual desire, both straight and lesbian, in national life.

My Fem Quest

For Barbara Cruikshank and Dianne Otto

The large hall of New York's Lesbian and Gay Community Center was dark in preparation for the night of benefit readings for ILGO (Irish Lesbian and Gay Organization). After climbing up four flights of stairs, I quietly slipped into the room and introduced myself to the young woman behind the table as one of the readers. "Oh, I know you, Joan," she whispered. "Look," she said, coming from behind the welcoming table and holding up her stockinged leg. "I wore these in your honor." Green pumps flashed in the darkness. How beautiful she was, in her short black dress, its hem hitting just above her knees.

Later in the evening, just as intermission was coming to an end and the room was darkening once again, a young woman appeared before me. Bending down so she could whisper her words to me, she said, "I had to come speak to you and thank you for what you have written about fems. You gave me the right to be myself." I looked up at her, at her neckline swinging away from her body, at her softly swelling breasts, such tender assertions, rising above a black lace bra, her dark curly hair framing her face so earnestly turned toward me. For one moment—I felt we were making love, the whispered voices, the darkened room, the revelation of the body—but this time I was the one struck by the gift of what she could offer. "Thank you," I mumbled, "but you are beautiful. You did not need any permission to be yourself."

The tensions between artifice and self, between enacting and being, between alienation and integration, between innocence and judgment were all present in those whispered words. I have emphasized youth in the retelling because two fem generations were represented that evening. How strange it was to be thanked for permission to return to the "natural" state of celebrating a young woman's body, adorning it in celebratory clothing. I think these younger women take play for granted, but it was "self" that was now the exciting creation.

I, on the other hand, am just beginning to understand that my fem desire, born in the 1950s or better said, expressed in the 1950s, can be explored in terms of performance as well as gut-wrenching need. My fem self is both an identity and a performance because I have outlived my own decades of risking all for a touch—meaning the vice squads, the police, the doctors—and now have the breathing space of some autonomy, both intellectually and politically, though I know how precarious this relief is. Because of my history, I have both a fem identity and a fem persona. And now I have something even more.

When I first started writing about my own sexual history, I thought being fem was as natural as breathing. While I also had a beginning understanding that all systems of desire have artifice built in—the glance, the body stance, the courtly gesture—it was the historical weight, the communal and yet somehow lonely courage of the butches and fems who stood with me in the darkness that was most real. Now I live and struggle in a world where nothing feels natural, where reality is constructed almost every day. I am still a little uneasy with the sometimes too glib and highly abstract language of postmodern theory, and I am grateful for a past that taught me early on when to be humble in the face of the sincerity of lives lived with so little protection and so much need. However, I am also learning that new positionings are a good thing.

In my introduction to *A Persistent Desire: A Femme-Butch Reader* (1992), I had naively suggested that the decade of the fem was upon us. I was wrong; I had not counted on the tremendous appeal of lesbian masculinity. I should have known better. In 1997, I attended two "cutting-edge" events on the subject of lesbian genders: one at the prestigious Whitney Museum, which had clearly discovered the chic in butch, and the other in the book-lined parlor of the Lesbian Herstory Archives. It soon became clear, however, at both these events, that only one gender was in full sight, the one I had taken delight in for so many years–butch and all its versions. At one of the events, a participant stated the familiar belief that a fem image by itself does not read as subversive; it would be perceived only as "woman." No matter how many times the groundbreaking work of Judith Butler and that of Sue-Ellen Case were referenced, I still felt that something was sadly familiar about this erasure of significance.

When I try to speak about what is missing from the postmodern discussion of lesbian genders, I find I have no language that feels comfortable, given all I know. For me, "fem" has a very problematic relationship to "femininity"; perhaps because I spent my early lesbian years as a butchy-looking fem, perhaps because I have lived my whole adult life within lesbian communities, or perhaps because my mother wanted me to be more her missing husband than her sexually competitive daughter and thus gave me only rudimentary instruction in how to be a girl–wear a girdle or your ass will look like the side of a barn, wear lipstick so you don't look like death, always be a good fuck.

For whatever reason, "femininity" carries a heterosexual

marker that does not signify what I mean when I speak of my femness. I have only the word *woman* to work with, but I do not know what this word means. I know I do not mean *woman* as in "woman-identified woman," or as in "lesbian woman" or as in the heterosexual term "woman." Somewhere in my construct of fem stands the full-bodied, big-breasted, big-assed woman, firm on her feet, taking in her lover's desire in the fulfillment of her own while she "works and works and works" (to quote Judy Grahn). It was always working-class clear to me that I had to earn my living in a very concrete way to make my erotic survival possible. Economics and my version of gender were inextricably tied.

(As I write these words, a shadow falls on me, the shadow of the Woman who toils in fields and factories, who walks endless miles for her family's water, who sits in the dust outside the clinic, her baby already exhausted with its struggle to live, the Woman "who has no place in Paradise," because she is too poor, too dark, too *woman*. I must never allow my pleasure with shifting terrains of meaning to carry me too far from her life or else I, too, become her tormentor.)

This questioning of all my layers of gender and sexual experience was forced upon me, in a wonderful way, by my friendship with younger, brave fems who are comfortable with discourse of all kinds. One woman in particular, Barbara Cruikshank, pursued me for a year to have a good sit-down with her and a tape recorder as we wrestled with our different fem histories. Barbara, whom I first met in San Diego when I was touring with *Persistent Desire*, is a compelling woman. Beautiful and sharp, she carries her own history of class deprivation into all her work without sacrificing her dreams of future accomplishment, her love affair with ideas, or her need for good hot butch-fem sex. When she suggested we collaborate on an inter-generational discussion of our fem lives, I knew I would be challenged by a different language and a less romantic vision of everything. I also knew that I would learn more about my fem self and how it would travel into the next century, if I am that lucky.

Barbara did not disappoint me. Her questions made me sort out the different threads of performance that created my experience of gender. "Are we making fems sound schizophrenic, girls with multiple personalities? Is that fem self different from what you call your woman self, and at what point in your day is this transition marked?" she relentlessly queried. For the first time, I looked at my actions and desires from a self-consciously postmodern point of view. I discovered layers of garments, of actions, of shifting terrains. When I moved through my day at school I did it as a "woman," professionally competent and loving to my students; my fem self was employed in the privacy of my relationship, in the security of my bed, under the gaze of my community. I said to Barbara that afternoon, "in my earlier years, being a fem made it bearable for me to be a woman."

We passed that afternoon, two women, with our heads bent low over the tape recorder, trying to pick out the threads of our fem lives. Barbara talked about our relationship to straight women and asked if we betrayed them when we took refuge in our fem selves. She wanted to know how fem transgressiveness is created, how can we make "being the girl" as hot as "being the boy." I gave my answers as best I could—not answers really, just words of exploration. My recognition of the complexity of my own erotic narrative could be a bridge between myself and straight women; it forced me to never conclude all was simple in any woman's story of her erotic choices and personas. We had no mutually agreed-upon answer for how we could imbue the fem image with the same kind of "cutting-edge" popularity the boygirl stance was engendering.

The weeks passed, and I grew a little uneasy with all the playing Barbara and I had done with our lives. I felt I had been seduced into an intellectual performance and while crucial, heartfelt ideas were raised, I was no more at ease with the central issue—how to honor, in the closing of this century, the woman who calls herself a fem. The more I think about it, the more it becomes clear to me that it is the concept of "woman" that is the sticking point. What to do with it? Is fem the performance, woman the essence? Is fem the parody, woman the false original category? Something is wrong with this whole discussion. My concern now is that behind all the sophisticated discussion of lesbian genders is a devaluing of the fem woman, not because she is fem but because she is a woman.

What kind of fem am I becoming? One who does not need to be on the arm of a butch-daddy-boygirl to have meaning and value in our world. One who takes great pleasure in the body of Bette Midler, in the memory of Simone Signoret, in the audacity of Gypsy Rose Lee, in the arms of another fem woman, in my own softness. I am the fem woman who has lived through the queer days, the butch-fem days, the lesbian-feminist days, and the queer days again; they are all part of this woman-fem that I am now. Now I stand alone, holding my body in my own hands, knowing that when I lie down with a butch lover, she is getting something precious, and when I take her cock in my mouth or her hand in my cunt, I do it as much to honor my own dreams as hers.

And to my woman-fem lover, who allowed me to love both her breasts and my own, whose body was so round like mine and as strong in its desire as mine, who allowed me to finally hold in my arms the world I had given to my butch lovers, I give the deepest kiss of recognition and of desire. All is possible, she says as she surges into me, and now finally, all is.

Note: This essay uses as its starting point a conversation with Barbara Cruikshank entitled "I'll Be the Girl: Generations of Fem," which appears in *Femme: Feminists, Lesbians and Bad Girls*, eds. Laura Harris and Elizabeth Crocker. New York: Routledge, 1997.

John Preston and Myself

July 9, 1964
Aurora, Colorado

Dear Bob,
I shouldn't have to tell you that your letter made me
cry. You are the only person I miss from Great
Falls–I miss talking with you and being with you.
It is much easier for me to say things by writing
them, and there is something I have wanted to tell
you for a long time. As a person, you are rare. I
don't know if you realize it or not, but it is almost
impossible for a girl to be a friend to a boy. *

I first met John Preston sometime in the early eighties when
we were on a panel of pornographers as part of a conference of gay and
lesbian journalists; a group of writers who had been censored for their
subject matter were meeting in one of the ground-floor rooms of the
newly opened Lesbian and Gay Center of New York City. I was the last

panel member to arrive, and I remember Pat Califia asking the whole panel to rise so I could wedge myself in behind the long table. John Preston was one of my colleagues on that day. He sat straight and tall, unflinching in his gaze, as he chronicled his career in erotic writing. Intrigued by his honesty and dedication to his writing, I began to read his books and keep an eye out for his name as he toured the country.

Over the years, I would get warm, encouraging cards from John, words that I needed in the face of some of the more ugly responses to my erotic writing. We were comrades in our dedication to telling the tales of how touch and taste and yearning encouraged life. My other good gay friends, Jonathan Katz and his lover David, Allan Berube, Bert Hansen, and Eric Garber, were all supportive of my history work, but it was John who read my books as portraits of sex.

In the mid-eighties, I grew aware of another dimension in John's work; he became one of the first creators of and spokespeople for a new eroticism: safer sex. He put his authoritative stance behind the possibility of hot, heavy gay male desire. Here we shared another parallel in our work. My erotic writings existed in a world where women lost their lives every day because of male violence. Every time I wrote of touch and entry, I had to weigh the consequences of my words. I had to ask myself if I was serving life, the fuller life of women, by breaking erotic silences. Both John and I chose to keep alive the taste, the power, of homoerotic desire.

In 1991, John started writing me letters about his idea for a book about relationships between gay men and lesbians. John was in love with the publishing world, and he was always looking for new projects that would please his agent and calm his relationship with the Internal Revenue Service. "Fondest of my Fantasies," he greeted me in one of his increasingly imploring letters, "it is time for us to get to work on this project." His salutations became more and more baroque as our correspondence grew: Dearest Love Goddess, Dearest Erotic Icon of My Soul, and finally, Dear Divine Being of My Groin. How could a girl resist? The letters themselves, after their courtly flourishes, showed the hard work of a professional writer. We both had other editing, speaking, and touring commitments that kept pushing at the time we had put aside for this book, but finally in 1992, John demanded that we find the time for the project that was to become *Sister and Brother: Lesbians and Gay Men Write About Their Lives Together.*

In the two years we worked together, I discovered more about John's history of activism in the gay community then I had ever known. I suggested that we hold a public conversation about why we wanted to write about the connected lives of gay men and lesbians in a celebratory way. I would write one section, and then John would answer. I am sure John found this a bit touchy-feely, but in his ever-courtly way, he bent over backward to accommodate me. Every new paragraph from him deepened my understanding of his journey–from his childhood in a small town in Massachusetts to his involvement in the civil rights movement in Boston, Chicago, and Montgomery, Alabama. He told how in 1969 he threw himself into the gay activism that was making Minneapolis a hotbed of queer organizing, founding the first gay and lesbian community center in the country–Gay House. In that city, he shared a house with Cindy Hansen, the lesbian co-director of Gay House, and her lover, Sharon. This experience of living with two lesbians and the long discussions he had with them about fathering a child with Sharon laid the basis for his willingness in the early 1990s to shatter some prevailing myths about relationships between gay men and lesbians. Not only had the specter of fatherhood raised itself in that shared house but complex sexual desires had also made themselves known.

John challenged me to write about my relationships with gay men in a way I could not have done in an earlier decade. Part of the price we had both paid in trying to create a public erotic voice was some simplification of our own erotic histories. My own relationships with gay men began in 1959 when I was attending Queens College, part of the City University of New York. Here in this working-class Berkeley of the East, I met Carl, the son of a trade unionist who had been purged from the union he had helped to organize in the first wave of red-bashing in the forties. Tall, broad, with a permanent cowlick over his forehead, Carl was part of a whole family of red-diaper babies who were studying such subjects as anthropology and psychology in the hopes of finding another way to keep the causes of the left alive.

This group of committed activists gave my own class anger a historical setting; my first date with Carl was to see Lotte Lenya portray Jenny in Brecht's *Threepenny Opera*, in a small Village theater. Afterward we sat in a huge and sparsely populated automat, where he explained Brecht's vision of the theater to me, the coffee cups piling up and the ashtray spilling over.

That night we attempted to make love as my mother slept in the next room. I was naked and Carl was stroking me, when my mother sleep-walked into the room. Carl threw his body over mine, and I said in a stern voice, "Mother, go back to sleep." Obediently, she turned herself around and marched back the way she had come. "What will I tell her in the morning?" I wondered out loud to Carl. "Tell her," he said quietly, "we were trying to find each other." All night we talked, not about Brecht or Joseph McCarthy but about Carl's first sexual experience with another man the night before and my own sexual explorations with women. We talked until the Queens sky turned orange with the new day; I still wanted Carl to make love to me, but I already knew that my womanness was not what he sought.

We kept our erotic searchings to ourselves while Carl and the others continued my cultural political education; hootenannies, early-morning gatherings in the deserted streets of Times Square to catch our bus to Washington, lessons in self-criticism, walks for peace, sit-downs for nuclear disarmament, training in how to survive tear gas attacks, which we needed to know for our protests against the Vietnam war, which carried us to the steps of the Pentagon. It was with these young people that I faced the uplifted bayonets of the National Guard for the first time. And while Carl and I did these actions together, while he taught me about the long tradition of radical protest in this country and introduced me to people like Paul Robeson, Jr., and Joanne Grant, we were also exploring how we could arouse each other's desire. I remember before one political meeting, wearing a sailor's cap as I made love to Carl, his long body stretched out before me. I spoke as if I were a young man and stroked his cock to arousal. Even in those early days, when sexual politics were not part of the leftist agenda, some of us sensed another knowledge waiting for its time. In 1992, in our talks and writings, John called these memories out of me.

At first our collaboration was marked by John's certainty about how to proceed. We used his agent, used his description of the goals of the book, used his list of gay male friends–and then, slowly, he grew weaker. His HIV status changed; the AIDS virus grew virulent, and I stepped in to take over the book. The tone of our conversations changed. Late at night, John would call me, furious at his loss of powers. I remember one night in particular when John wept on the phone, saying that he had turned down a gay video maker's request that John allow himself to filmed. "I am not going to be just another faggot dying on film," he said. "I want to be remembered as the young boys saw me, the author of those hot books." I had no easy words for my dear companion other than to assure him that the book would get done.

In 1993, John was making one final round of the New York publishers to sell his autobiography, and he stopped off to visit me and my lover. Sprawling on our couch, John extended his long legs far out into the living room. Our dog, sensing his love of the species, curled at John's feet. It was a sweltering summer day. This was the first time John met Lee, my partner, who is a devoted fan of his Mr. Benson series. From across the room, I noticed how they resembled each other–both lean and gray, both marked by the slate blue of their eyes. John was tired and upset at the lack of interest in his proposed autobiography. He repeated the words of an influential editor he had just spoken to: "You know, Preston, the story of a middle-aged gay man fighting AIDS is not news anymore."

John's retelling of this encounter brought back to me a conversation I'd had a few months earlier when I called a Jewish archives to see if they would be interested in receiving a copy of my neighbor's story of how he had survived the ghetto of Riga. I had worked with David, now a man in his seventies, as he translated his original Yiddish text into English. David sat by my side as I typed his journey of loss, of flight, of resistance into my computer, stopping only when his grief overcame his words. He had insisted that his story must be remembered, beyond the confines of his immediate family, and so I made the call to a likely place. "Miss Nestle," the weary voice of the archivist informed me, "I know you find this story very impressive, very dramatic, very unique, but I am saddened to have to tell you that we already have thousands of such stories."

The afternoon after John's visit was the opening of the new Brooklyn home of the Lesbian Herstory Archives. Again the heat blared down, but I was so excited by the crowds of women, by the beauty of our new space, that I just plunged ahead. Through the streets of the Brooklyn's Park Slope we marched, our own small band drumming us along, over four hundred celebrants jamming into a building in Prospect Park to hear speeches, to eat, and, of course, to dance. I ran from table to table along with the other archives workers, making sure the chaos was pleasurable for our guests. Finally too tired, too hot to keep up the hectic scurrying, I stopped and just looked around at the moving, swirling mass of lesbians celebrating their own cultural institution. Then I saw John, his head towering above most of the crowd, standing with sweat dripping down him, his luggage pulling at his arms. I made my way toward him. "I just had to come," he said. "I knew how important this was to you. I can't stay; I have to make a train home." He bent his head so I could kiss him good-bye and I felt his fever, like another sweltering August day, burning inside of him.

One place John and I counted on seeing each other was at the annual OutWrite conference, a gathering of queer writers, editors, and readers. The conference of 1993 was our last chance to solicit manuscripts for our book, so we had several work-related meetings. One of these took place in the main lobby of the Boston hotel that opened its endless rooms to the almost two thousand OutWrite participants who poured out over its corridors and coffee shops. A favorite gathering spot was a small bar and lounge on a raised platform in the bustling lobby. Here I joined John, who was seated in the center of a small couch; on either side of him were men, some young, some not, some California sun-tanned, some New York weary. I joined this circle and, for a short time, shared in what was John's world. The talk was about the previous evening's party for John's new *Flesh and the Word* anthology and the erotic adventures that flowed from it. The men teased each other, encouraged each other, and made promises to stay in touch. Even though the men were speaking to each other, they all sat half-turned to John, who from time to time told them a story about a man he had made love to there...here... His voice hoarse and weary, he spoke again about the traveling salesman who had inaugurated him into the power and joy of sex many years ago, close by to the very hotel in which we were now sitting. In my younger years, I would have been uncomfortable in this setting, lost in my difference, but now in my mid-fifties, secure in that very difference, I was content to listen to the stories, the erotic gossip that was laced with love. I soon understood that the men were paying their homage to John, that they were thanking him for years of writing about and work for the gay male body and its travels.

Later that same day at OutWrite, a small group of us squeezed in a trip to the park that bordered the hotel so that a photographer could take publicity photos of John and me. Huddled against the November wind, John and I positioned ourselves on a bench, trying to find poses with which we both felt comfortable. Finally I gave up trying to find the pose that would not call up stereotypical male-female images and just let my body find its own position. I knew I wanted to hold John, for my own self, and so I raised myself up and held his head against my breast. Immediately, I became aware of his fever, of the heat emanating from his body. Several months later when I saw the finished photos, I was struck by how our hands had found a way to hold on to each other's bodies.

Back in my hotel room that night, I wondered at how John Preston, New England gay man, and Joan Nestle, Bronx fem Jew, had ended up on that Boston bench together. Our need to write about sex, to have sex, our long histories of community struggle, our delight in the published word, even the growing frailty of our own bodies had drawn us into each other's worlds. I do not fool myself into thinking that I knew John Preston well; I did not. I do not fool myself into thinking I was one of the public personas, like Anne Rice, on whose support and style he thrived. I was not. But we had traveled some roads together. He, like me, had insisted that flesh could find its words, and he insisted on giving his readers the sweetness of palpable desire.

> *Denver, Colorado*
> *December 12, 1964*

> *My darling, my darling Bob:*
> *Your magnificent letter! I kissed it and tried to think how I could convey in words the love I feel for you. There is no way I can tell you how much I need you in my life–don't ever step out of it.*

*The excerpts from the Colorado letters are part of a special collection documenting the friendship between a lesbian and a gay man in the 1960s. Donated to the Lesbian Herstory Archives by Robert Cunningham, who died in 1997.

III.
Our Gift of Touch

Our Gift of Touch

When I was asked to speak about women's history to women confined in the women's prison in Kingston, Ontario, Canada, I wanted to bring the lesbians in the prison a gift, so I wrote this piece as a broadside that could be handed out. I wanted to honor lesbian sex in prison, to honor the women who wanted each other, not because there were no men available but because they were lesbians. Unfortunately, once the group leader who had invited me into the prison announced to the gathered women and their teachers that I was going to speak about lesbian history, the head teacher decided that I was an inappropriate speaker for the two hundred women and marched them out. Ten women managed to stay, and it was they who distributed the broadside to the women in prison who wanted it.

My life has taught me that touch is never to be taken for granted, that a woman reaching for my breasts or parting my legs is never a common thing, that her fingers finding me or her tongue taking me are not mysterious acts to be hidden away but that all of it, the embraces, the holdings-on, the moans, the words of want, are acts of sunlight. I still watch with amazement your head between my legs, seeing the length of you, all the years of you, reaching for my pleasure. How in such a world as this, where guns and governments crush tenderness every day, can you find your way to that small, hidden woman's place? But you do, intent and knowing; you make the huge need come.

How can I ever grow accustomed to the beauty of your cheek against my breast, or the protective strength with which you turn me over? How can I ever think it ordinary, your desire to caress the tighter places, to take the time to calm me and then to help me want what I cannot see? Or how you reach for me after I have pleasured you, pulling me up along your body, your fingers gently cleaning my lips, which glisten with your taste. Or how you make a pillow of your shoulder, to comfort me after the coming.

Never will I take for granted in this world your generosity of exploration, how you have listened to my body and found what you could do, and the way you surprise me with it when I come to bed and reach for you and feel the leather straps around your waist. You never announce, you simply smile and do.

Never will I take for granted the miracle of your desire to comfort me, the trips you have taken to reach me, late at night, appearing at my door in your jeans and T-shirt, coming like the morning. Or when you stand beside me, bare-breasted, clothed only in your leather jacket and white socks, your small belly pushing forward, your eyes glinting at the depth of my response. How all stands still at that moment, and all the losses of time and all the fears of night fall at your feet. Or the times you have held me against your heart, telling me it was alright to cry for everything.

The only shame I ever feel now, after so many years of women's touch, is never saying thank you enough.

My life has taught me that touch is never to be taken for granted, that a woman reaching for my breast or parting my legs is never a common thing.

A Fem's Diary

The snow falls softly outside the high small windows of our little apartment atop an old Provincetown gray shingled house. We see it mix with the sea gulls and the tops of the bare trees and then float past us to a lower place we do not see. I have asked her to dress for me, and she comes out of the bathroom in her lavender negligee with a lace jacket thrown over her shoulders. Her hair is down in full life, spreading out around her face. She has put on deep red lipstick; her eyes glisten with touches of color. Perfumes reach me first, and I tighten with desire. She is smiling, her taunting smile, her knowing smile that denies her twenty-eight years. When she is this way, so splendid in her largeness and beauty, I feel my years drop away. I am younger, far younger than this woman who has the knowledge of body painting, of how to hold her long legs so the gown reaches mid-thigh but no higher.

I ask her to lie down on the couch, and I get a pillow for the back of her head so she will be comfortable. As she places herself on the couch, the jacket opens and her full breasts are exposed to me. I have already left my mark on one of them, a large brown mark left by my teeth and my relentless mouth that has such need of her. I stay at the opposite end of the couch from her, resting my head on her knee, one of her legs stretched out alongside of me. She slowly starts caressing her breast, fingering her nipples, daring me to touch her. She pushes my hand away every time I try. I learn to wait, but waiting is also pleasure because I have her legs, her calf and thighs to caress, to run my lips over their smoothness, to smell her powder and her sex as I push my head into her lap. She laughs at me, at my adoration, as she rumples my hair. She laughs at me as I grip her full, gowned body in my woman's hands.

Then I can no longer play. I push her hands away and she gives me her breasts. I find her under the gown and raise her legs up over my shoulders. My fingers find her open and I push into her, watching her face all the time, the heaving of her breasts. I am fully clothed but naked in my want, in my imagination, in my need to be her lover. I grasp the cock I have chosen, the biggest, the longest one that will give her the most pleasure, and while her legs are on my shoulders, I enter her with it, first slowly and deeply and then quicker and harder, my body behind each thrust. Her legs are now bent, her knees almost on her breasts. She is moving and moaning, holding me to her—and then as if her body were mine, I sense the tiredness of her legs and pull out. I let her legs drop and she smiles, "Thank you." I lie over her, my face buried in her neck.

She starts to touch herself, almost as if she is afraid I will not know her need. But I do. I spend long minutes, long, wonderful moments buried in her cunt, my cheeks caressed by her hanging gown, sucking her into me, always smelling the perfume of her body, of her anointing.

Later I will play old whore to her younger girl. I will wear my black slip and stockings and she will wear her white undershirt with a little ribbon over her breasts. And after I have taught this woman what she wants to know, the pleasure of ass fucking, she will plead for the right to touch me, and then my own fem need will come flooding back, and she will hold me in her arms, saying quietly, "Joan, I want to fuck you," and all her perfume will be part of her strength as she enters me with her long fingers dipped in red, not riding me but pushing me to let go. "Fuck my fingers, fuck my fingers," she urges.

To me, she appears as nothing other than a woman, but in my mind's passion, I have been boy, older man, aging whore, woman. I am grateful for the height of our windows, that the only witnesses to our moments are the clouds and falling snow, not because of shame but because they speak of dreams, of certainties loosened from their moorings, dreams of desire and touch that we have shared. I have held cocks and a woman who reminded me of my mother dressed for her lover, and I have been her lover. I have taken my own womanness and used it as a teacher for this beautiful and caring woman.

After J. leaves, the sadness descends. I read the papers every day in this hiding-away place. I mourn for D., have nightmares of screaming at her, I wonder what worth I am to my students. Perhaps all the fucking, all the nuances are hopeless. Governments with their pale men in suits kill and flaunt and designate despair. Where could such a shifting exchange between two women, one twenty years older than the other, have meaning other than among the clouds of a village at the edge of the sea?

My Woman Poppa

You work at a job that makes your back rock-hard strong; you work with men in a cavernous warehouse loading trucks while others sleep. Sometimes when you come to me, when my workday is just beginning, you fall asleep in my bed on your stomach, the sheet wrapped around your waist, the flaming unicorn on your right shoulder catching the morning sun.

I just stand and look at you, at your sleeping face and square, kind hands, my desire growing for you, for my woman poppa who plays the drums and knows all the words to "Lady in Red," who calls me sassafras mama, even when I am too far from the earth, who is not frightened off by my years or my illness.

My woman poppa who knows how to take me in her arms and lie me down, knows how to spread my thighs and then my lips, who knows how to catch the wetness and use it, who knows how to enter me so waves of strength rock us both.

My woman poppa who is not afraid of my moans or my nails

but takes me and takes me until she reaches beyond the place of entry into the core of tears. Then as I come to her strength and woman fullness, she kisses away my legacy of pain. My cunt and heart and head are healed.

My woman poppa who does not want to be a man, but who travels in "unwomanly" places and who does "unwomanly" work. Late into the New Jersey night, she maneuvers the forklift to load the thousands of pounds of aluminum into the hungry trucks that stand waiting for her. Dressed in the shiny tiredness of warehouse blue, with her company's name stitched in white across her pocket, she endures the bitter humor of her fellow workers, who are men. They laugh at Jews, at women, and when the black workers are not present, at blacks. All the angers of their lives, all their dreams gone dead, bounce off the warehouse walls. My woman grits her teeth and says when the rape jokes come, "Don't talk that shit around me."

When she comes home to me, I must caress the parts of her that have been worn thin, trying to do her work in a man's world. She likes her work, likes the challenge of the machines and the quietness of the night, likes her body moving into power.

My woman poppa is thirteen years younger than I, but she is wise in her woman-loving ways. Breasts and ass get her hot, that wonderful hot which is a heard and spoken desire. I make her hot, and I like that. I like her sweat and her tattoos. I like her courtliness and her disdain of the boys. I mother her and wife her and slut her, and together we are learning to be comrades.

She likes me to wear a black slip to bed; to wear dangling earrings and black stockings with sling-back heels when we play. She likes my perfume and lipstick and nail polish. I enjoy these slashes of color, the sweetened place in my neck where she will bury her head when she is moving on me.

I sometimes sit on her, my cunt open on her round belly, my breasts hanging over her, my nipples grazing her lips. I forbid her to touch me and continue to rock on her, my wetness smearing her belly. She begins to moan and curves her body upward, straining at the restrictions.

"Please baby, please," my woman poppa begs. "Please let me fuck you." Then suddenly, when she has had enough, she smiles, opens her eyes, and says, "You have played enough." Using the power she has had all along, she throws me from my throne.

Sometimes she lies in bed wearing her cock under the covers. I can see its outline under the pink spread. I just stand in my slip watching her, her eyes getting heavy. Then I sit alongside her, on the edge of the bed, telling her what a wonderful cock she has, as I run my hand down her belly until I reach her lavender hardness. I suck her nipples and slowly stroke her, tugging at the cock so she can feel it through the leather triangle that holds it in place.

"Let me suck you," I say, my face close to hers, my breasts spilling out on hers. "Let me take your cock in my mouth and show you what I can do." She nods, almost as if her head were too heavy to move.

Oh, my darling, this play is real. I do long to suck you, to take your courage into my mouth, both cunt, your flesh, and cock, your dream, deep into my mouth, and I do. I throw back the covers and bend over her carefully so she can see my red lips as I move on her. I give her the best I can, licking the lavender cock its whole length and slowly tangoing the tip, circling it with my tongue. Then I take her fully into my mouth, into my throat. She moans, moves, tries to watch and cannot as the image overpowers her. When I have done all that I can, I bend the wet cock up on her belly and sit on her so I can feel it pressing against my cunt. I rock on her until she is ready, and then she reaches down and slips the cock into me. Her eyes are open now, wonderfully clear and sharp. She slips her arms down low around my waist so I am held tight against her. Very slowly, she starts to move her hips upward in short strong thrusts. I am held on my pleasure by her powerful arms; I can do nothing but move and take and feel. When she knows I have settled in, she moves quicker and quicker, her breath coming in short, hard gasps. But I hear the words "Oh baby, you are so good to fuck."

I forget everything but her movements. I fall over her, my head on the pillow above her. I hear sounds, moans, shouted words, know my fists are pounding the bed, but I am unaware of forming words or lifting my arms. I ride and ride harder and faster, encircled by her arms, by her gift.

"Give it all to me, let it all go," I know she is saying. I hear a voice answering, "you you you you" and I am pounding the bed, her arms, anything I can reach. How dare you do this to me, how dare you push me beyond my daily voice, my daily body, my daily fears. I am chanting; we are dancing. We have broken through.

Then it is over. We return, and gently she lifts off her belly. I slide down her body, rest, and then release her from the leather. We sleep.

Yes, my woman poppa knows how to move me, but she knows many other things as well. She knows she will not be shamed; she knows her body carries complicated messages. She knows that breast and cock and cunt are shaped by dreams. My woman poppa, my dusty sparrow, how special you are.

Woman of Muscle, Woman of Bone

For Lee Hudson

Her body covered me with a cape of muscled strength. Her voice, that controlled, trained voice, found another register, and she said my name in long expulsions of breath. With each emptying of her lungs, she lunged her knee between my legs, pushing my large, full thighs farther apart. I was on my stomach under her, my head turned on the pillow, my sweat marking the tension of being so completely held. Each time she pulled herself up for another thrust, I could see her. Just the tip of her. Her short gray hair, her neck swollen with her exertions but made delicate by the beaded necklace that hung just away from the thickened muscle. Then the push would come, and I could see nothing. My whole body absorbed the impact through my cunt that was so wet it dripped upon the sheets, up into my stomach and into my breasts, which shook and grew larger under the impact. My whole body absorbed that one move and braced for the next.

My arms were stretched out on either side of me; her hands gripped my own. In the pauses between her mountings, I pressed my lips against the hardness of her forearms, against the cords of muscle. I tried to bite into her flesh, but there was no skin that hung freely. All was stretched to its limit to cover the swell of muscle. Like the corded ropes of a ship's railing, her arms kept me from falling, and I turned my cheek into her hardness, caressing the safety of her muscles.

She has worked very hard for each ridge, each swell of sculptured flesh. Sometimes while I lie in bed waiting for her, I imagine her in the gym where she has chosen to wage the battle against smallness. I can see her in her gray sweatpants and white T-shirt, sitting on a bench, her legs spread wide into a V, her back arched, her body tilted over her working arm and her left hand braced on her inner thigh. She curls her arm over and over, the weights like Sisyphean stones she cannot let go. Her head is turned in a concentrated stare as if to will the muscle into new growth, her repeated movements a chant against the body's frailty.

After innumerable curls, she moves on to her next and next task, always weighing her body down, so resistance itself becomes both a comrade and an enemy. Here in this mirrored place, women's bodies bend in a devoted dance, pushing and pulling their flesh into newly muscled forms.

Finally in this dream, I come to her when she is drenched in sweat and finished with the endless battle for this day. I come to her and stand before her, my body soft, full, and marked with aging. I push her back against the wall. She falls into it as if its hardness were a pillow. I run my hands over her trembling muscles, over her almost breastless chest where flesh has fled. I find her nipples, the pouting remnants, and I tease them over and over again, forcing her to feel another kind of muscle tightness.

When her nipples are hard knots, I reach up and force her head down so she has to see my red nails flagrantly decorative, outlining her ridges. I deepen their touch so her muscle is indented by fem persistence. My hands move over her belly, now transformed into a thick egg resting in a nest of bone. I stay on her belly for a long time, pushing, caressing, circling its firmness until she moves forward from the wall, pushing her hips toward me. So much yearning in the bone.

I push her back, letting her know I will not accept her impatience. Soon her breath quickens and a new sheen of sweat shines upon her skin. I lean forward and lick drops of her body's wetness off her chest, lingering in the hollow of her throat. Now she knows what I will do, and all her strength cannot stop me. I stand straight in front of her, close but not resting on her. She senses my certainty, smells my perfume, and tenses.

"You know what I am going to do."

Her head turns, following the words. Her eyes are still closed.

"Oh Joan, oh God," she implores. My hand moves down to her hips, to her lower belly, to her thighs. I peel off her pants as I travel, letting them fall to her ankles. She stands naked before me. Her body is arched, hungry, tight. I enjoy all that I see with a deep appreciation for her work and with delight at what I can bring her. I move closer, my breath touching her. After a silence, a protracted moment of suspended action, I cup her cunt in my hand. Her wetness is already seeping through. My red nails are petals of crimson against her wiry hair. Now she rests in my palm, her smallest muscle throbbing in my hand. My body moves behind each rubbing, pushing her harder against the wall, pushing her into her own rhythm of want. Suddenly, knowing she is ready, I seize her turned head and with a quick move, enter her, reminding her of the waiting, wanting, softness beneath the bone.

This was my dream as I lay in the bed waiting for her, my fantasy of gratitude and appreciation. Now she appears wearing her white cotton gi, her body oiled and laced with beads of water. Like two ancient wrestlers, we assume our positions: I on my stomach and she lowered upon me. The weight of her is pushing the dream from my mind, but I remember the power of my taking and I feel a surge of my own resistance. My refusal is to be just a body under her that takes her strength without a voice of its own.

Throughout the days of my life, I too have built muscle. My body tightens under her. I harden the center of my back and push up against her, carrying her whole long body with me, announcing my refusal to be intimidated by her strength. Her delight at my resistance, expressed in low laughter that turns to moans, gives me the victory I want. She hangs against my ass, pushing herself into it, trying to get more and more of it against herself. For a moment, I hold both of us, our weights now joined. I balance on my elbows. My head bends low between my breasts, which have fallen out of my nightgown. I am now my own kind of athlete. She is marooned above the bed, lifted high on my back, curled over my fullness.

She pushes, rocks, groans, and then there is silence. I know what is coming. I can almost hear her body laughing as she reaches under me. If she feels kind, she pushes out one elbow and then the other until I fall with a rush, flat on my stomach. When she is more impatient, she simply takes me down and places her hand between my shoulder blades, like an anchor, while with the other, she reaches inside of me, bringing me home on waves of strong, steady movement.

Woman of muscle, woman of bone, I have not known your kind before.

The Uses of Strength

1

She stood in front of me, her sweatpants low around her hips, her nipples hard. I arose from my bed and just leaned my head against the side of her thigh, and then as if I were climbing a ladder up out of my exhaustion, I stretched up toward her, moving my hand from the curve of her belly up to her chest, where it lay, fingers splayed out along her ribs. I rested there until I became aware of the fluttering of her heart, and then I hurried on. Soon my cheek was against hers, and though she stood, and I kneeled on the bed I had come to know too well, I was her equal in the travels of the flesh.

2

We had driven up the coast to Gloucester on a gray spring day. She had wanted to visit the hometown of a poet she admired, but before we reached the small New England city, we came upon a park that overlooked the ocean. We walked slowly over the soggy earth until we reached a cliff that fronted the sea. She stood in front of me, catching the full force of the wind, her gray hair dancing in the autumn air. I stood behind her, leaning against her back, my arms around her waist. The ocean rolled in, over and over, gray and complete and never still. I began to cry for all the oceans I had seen with lovers, for all the leave-takings that had left their marks around my heart.

3

If I take you in my arms, pull your head to my breasts, if I curve my hand over the winged blades of your back, pressing you farther into me, if I spread my legs to give you better purchase, settling your bones into my flesh, if I move into you, gripping your want with my openness, if I press my mouth against your neck, my tongue softening the skin where my teeth will pull at you, if I slide down your narrow belly, my breasts dragging against your skin, if I bury my face in your cunt, spreading your lips with my tongue, if I take all of you into my mouth, sucking the folds open, if I push two fingers into you, pulling at your pleasure, if I swirl my tongue over your swollen clit when your muscles tightening around my fingers tell me you are ready to come, if I close up your lips while you are still pulsing so you can keep the sweetness longer, if I pull myself up alongside your body and rest my head on your shoulder as your breathing slows down and the sweat dries on your breasts—will you think I am weak?

4

I turned my cheek against the rough wall, my hands stretched out above my head, trying to find a hold. I felt the coldness of the wall in my belly. "Close your eyes," she insisted quietly, pressing into me. She spread my legs with one of hers, her leathered leg pushing my slip up until my ass was bare. I pushed farther into the wall, wanting to escape my own nakedness. I could hear footsteps all around me as other women moved through the narrow passageways of the bar's back room. Her gloved hand moved over my hips; my slip fell off my shoulders, but I had to let it go. My hands could not leave the wall. No rope was needed, no scarlet tie. Years of shame pinned me to the wall, while air moved over my nakedness. I waited, and then she returned, fully. Her hand curved over my ass, leaving only to deliver sharp, short spanks, and then to knead the never-seen, never-wanted flesh, until a heat ran down the back of my thighs, a heat that made me spread my legs even more because pure want was pouring out of me. She laughed against my ear and then entered me, pushing at my tightness until resistance became a sweetness. After she left, I turned around in the darkness, too tired to move off the wall. Pulling my slip down, I faced the passing women, my comrades, quietly and directly.

5

The nights are hard. Often sleep does not come. She turns to me, gazing quietly at my desperation. Her hand reaches out and for long minutes, she strokes my breasts, my belly, my legs. I move into the crook of her arm and soon her heartbeat, slow and steady, becomes my own.

A Feeling Comes

*The title is adapted from an Emily Dickinson poem,
"After great pain, a formal feeling comes–"*

I lay quietly, thinking of ways to bear the pain. If I kept perfectly still, the terrible aching would become a dull throb, a constant warning of the power of a renewed attack. So much of being ill is a matter of bargains, of negotiations with the seen and the unseen in an endless attempt to appease the spirit of the illness and gain the kindness of strangers.

For many years, I had lived in a world of whispered prayers, heard only by me, trying to ward off further humiliations of the body. I knew I could always take the painkillers waiting on the overloaded night table. Surrounded by books and glasses of water, the little bottle carried the promise of the dissolution of feeling and thought. It beckoned me to a climate where a soft fog dominated the landscape. I had already spent two days, flat on my back, traveling between the mist-shrouded peace of this land and the rocky murmurings of pain. I now chose to decline its passport.

Tonight I was lucky. I was not alone. I could hear Lee preparing something in the kitchen. A few minutes later, she appeared in the doorway, carrying a steaming cup of tea.

"Here, darling. I know you think tea is tinted hot water, but try this."

She made room on the night stand, pushing away the debris of illness, and sat on the edge of the bed.

"I have to go soon, but I hate leaving you this way."

Just the weight of her on my bed gave me hope. I reached out and took her hand. "I'm sorry we did not have more good time together. Our weekends are so precious. I'm so sorry."

I could feel the tears coming, the words of regret for being this burden in her life, but the sight of her, trying so hard to help, stopped my outburst. Instead, I pulled her closer, delighting in her gray eyes, direct and yet struggling to be hopeful, her smaller body, which the world would call boyish even if she was close to fifty. I touched her with my eyes and she smiled, relaxing a little. Encouraged, I began to unbutton her shirt; she held perfectly still while I uncovered the swell of her breasts. I let her sit there, just like that, in the still room for a long moment. Then she laughed and returned my challenge by throwing back the cover and teasing my nipples so even the flannel nightgown could not contain my excitement. I took her hand, which had given me so much delight in our time together, and brought it to my mouth, running the back of it over my lips, tracing its veins with my tongue. All the while, we were with our eyes, giving permissions and wondering how far we could go. I let go of bargains and prayers. I no longer feared the pain.

"I want to make love before you go...don't say no, I want to take back part of what we have lost."

"But can we?" Lee questioned, even as I pushed her off the bed. Very carefully, keeping my head and back as straight as I could, I left the bed and walked toward the closet. Hanging on an outside hook was my black nightgown, the one that excited Lee the most because its lace panels exposed just enough to make her want more. I left her standing next to the bed as I marched out of the room.

Dressed for desire, I stood before my lover, who was once again sitting of the edge of the bed, her head bowed.

"Darling, here, I am here."

I lifted her head up and stroked back her hair. Lee moved her face into my breasts, then into my belly. She wrapped her arms around me and pushed me forward so her tongue could push through the lace. For a minute, the pain sprang up, lashing its tail, but my belly swelled with want, and I refused to turn back. Lee reached for my breasts, teasing my nipples until they made their own way through the labyrinth of lace. With closed eyes, she moved from nipple to nipple, sucking them into her mouth, her tongue rolling them over and over. I heard her sighs and felt her strength, I soon had to pull away.

"Honey, are you okay?" she breathed into my belly.

"I will show you how well I am doing," I said in that playfully serious way we had that signaled I was going to deliver an erotic order. "I am going to lie down and you are going to sit on my face so I can taste you."

For a minute Lee looked concerned and then she realized that I had found a way to accommodate both pain and pleasure. She stood up and I lay back down on the bed, a bed made different by our touch. I spread myself out for her, fanning the gown around me. My hips recognized the change first and began to ride the bed, very slowly but very surely. My thighs, which had been so heavy in the flannel, woke to their power. I lifted one leg so Lee could see my want.

"Come closer," I commanded, and when she did, I reached out and began to unzip her dungarees, stopping from time to time to push my hand against her. Lee took this for as long as she could and then pushed my hand away and stepped out of her pants.

For one moment, she stood there, looking down at me, her

belly bare, her sex lips clearly visible through her hair, and then she straddled me, but still careful, keeping her weight on her knees. She bent to kiss me, and I grabbed her tongue with my need, my hands caught on her arms. Finally, she lowered herself onto my belly and I could feel her sex on me, warming my body. I gently moved under her, rocking her against me, letting her ride each wave. Her breath came more quickly, and I curved my body upward, pushing against the pain, pushing for her, moving her up to my lips. She reached behind me, putting a small pillow under my head so I did not have to strain to taste her. Using the wall as her brace, she lowered herself onto my lips.

All was dark in the room now, but caught between her thighs I found bright worlds of taste and smell. In gratitude, I reached up and grasped her breasts, which were hanging over me like small fruits. From far off I heard her moans, but closer I heard the roar of waters. I reached my tongue farther into her, finding such multitudes of taste and texture, sweetness and salt, curves and walls, hair sharp and flesh rounded and wet that I could not stop my travels. All of her was poised on my mouth, a world of a woman held on my tongue, and I was rolling pleasure into her. Soon, too soon, she threw back her head and shouted.

Silence returned to us, and as I opened my eyes and she lifted off me, I could see my pain advancing toward us–its head bowed in tribute.

The Ridge Runners

A lesbian couple who, like us, were summer inhabitants of this Catskill region, came by for an afternoon lunch by our pond, bringing with them a friend who had visited the summer before. The attraction between my lover and this young woman, a teacher-artist who painted huge canvases in her downtown loft, was palpable in the summer air. The young artist swirled around us in an earth-colored sarong and halter top, her skin sun browned, muscle and breast all swollen with victories. In a moment of playfulness, she removed her skirt and then pushed my jock lover into the cold waters of the pond, diving in after her to make sure her conquest was complete.

I heard their shouts and turned to see Lee, my lover, climbing out of the pond, standing with water dripping off her lean, muscular body, shorts and T-shirt plastered against her flesh, hair flattened against her head. She stood there half-stunned by the audacity of our guest. The young woman, continuing her challenge, danced a few steps away from her, half poised to flee.

This is what I saw and what I knew. My lover would have this woman, not in that late-summer afternoon light, but in a darkened room somewhere back in the city. I was older than the newcomer by twenty years and had been ill. Illness, like floods, washes away the simply loose things first, and then it pushes at the bedrock. Too many nights I had turned away from Lee's desire. Anger, sickness, disappointments, and hurt rose like a wall between us, and while Lee could still make love to me, I did all I could to numb myself to her. For her, desire meant strength and reaffirmation of self; for me, it meant weakness and loss. Yet I wanted everyone to know what a wonderful lover she was, and as if she were a superb possession I could no longer use, I offered her to others.

I told her that I understood her need, that it was alright if she had an affair. I thought it was. I would be the slowed-down older woman who with great noblesse oblige handed over her still-vital lover to the passion she herself could not provide. Old Bette Davis movies were running through my mind; elegantly bereft, I would be. In control of things, I would be. But watching their foreplay in the summer heat, I began to feel uneasy with my own scenarios.

Later that afternoon, the three of us planned a journey up the mountainside to find a secret waterfall that Clarence Hartwell, the elderly farmer who was our neighbor, had told us was hidden in the folds of the mountain. As a young boy, he had taken delight in running barefooted over the ridges of the surrounding hills. "I would rather run then eat when I was hungry," he had told us one morning earlier in the summer, challenging us to retrace his youthful discoveries.

That day was hot and heavy. We made our way through the meadow, lit by an almost unbearable sun until we reached the beginning of the forest. The stream was just a short distance ahead of us, and we had our first choice to make—to follow the riverbed or to go along the bank. I chose the riverbed, they chose the bank.

In its first meandering, the stream was easy to travel on.

I stepped from stone to stone, looking down at the river bottom, hoping to see some exotic river creature. Then the stream narrowed, and the footing became more treacherous. Several times I slipped into the cold water, reaching out to grab at a branch or tree trunk to keep myself from falling.

At one point, the younger woman came back to me, offering to help me over some especially rocky places. At first I was grateful, but then I wanted to push her away, push away her perfect body, her kindness based on sureness. "I know about you and Lee," I said at one resting place.

"I knew you would understand," she said. "You write so beautifully about passion, you of all people would understand." My breath stopped for a minute. I did not tell her that my body was breaking. I nodded and sent her on. For a long while I rested, breathing in the damp smells of the streambed and sipping water from my cupped hand.

For an hour, I traveled in the heart of the stream. No part of it escaped me. Slowly I was climbing the mountain. My two fellow explorers, walking on higher ground, had left me far behind. I could hear their shouts through the trees, "Here, it turns here." Soon I had to climb more slowly, clutching at whatever the bank offered me by way of support.

My lover's shouts alerted me to their discovery. I looked up and saw them both standing high on the edge of a huge stone outcropping, far above me. Now I was crawling up the mountainside, my head close to the moss-covered earth, my fingers digging into water-softened rootbeds. Ancient smells of mold enveloped me. Above, massive stone slabs like giant steps formed the basic structure of the falls. This hard old break in the mountain's side, its waters gushing out all around us, was the ridge runner's secret.

When I finally joined Lee and her new lover and sat with them, our feet dangling over the edge of the flat black rock, I knew that whatever fantasies I had entertained about being in control of their mutual desire had been ground out of me.

Now, far from me, they are consummating the need that flared up on the way to the waterfall, the young dark woman, all bared desire, and my lover, ready to answer the call. On the way back from the falls, they fell far behind me on the trail, and as I made my way over the now-familiar riverbed, I lost sight and sound of them. Younger and stronger than me, they had fallen behind–to look for fossils, they would say. I did not look back; I did not want to see the kiss or the hurried touch. I had given away my lover one time too many.

The water in the stream was low, tired in the late summer, but I had seen its source, seen the ancient table of stone over which it had journeyed for thousands of years. I had dipped my hand into its stone cradle of caught water. How could I make sense of all of this–my own scheming against myself, the beauty of their physical love, the enduring wetness of the seeping earth? On the way home, I was not as careful in my footsteps. I walked resolutely away from the silenced excitement behind me.

Now my lover is entering the young woman, her muscles bunched up in her arm, her intense face hanging over the woman below her. She will push at her, in her. She will not stop until she has completely exhausted the woman under her. She is that kind of lover, relentless, self-less, and yet she grows big with each thrust.

I am back in the city. All the bittersweet dramas of the summer are behind me. Mr. Hartwell and his stories of floods and late night run-ins with the ghosts of the mountains have been replaced by the gritty reality of sirens blaring and the loneliness of my room when I know my lover is elsewhere. Now the words come pouring out of me. I re-create their sex play, a drama I know so well, as if my words could carry me into their passion, into their gathered intensity, where all is concentrated muscle and thrusting hips. How I have fooled myself, and how careless I was of Lee's offerings.

I will write a story about how it all happened, how the summer and the water and an old farmer and his boyhood habit of running over the hills gave us pieces of meaning, how they led us from a half-buried cemetery where bones picked clean of passion were growing down deeper and deeper into the earth to a scar in the ridgetops that poured forth endless, and sometimes sad, possibilities.

I used to run over the hills too, the hills of lovers' bodies, the mountains of touch. I had made trails for myself in bedrooms and bars, a young girl wanting and always saying more, please more.

Now I sit, as the night grows later, in a room in the city trying to put up words to stand against the flood of knowledge and of memory, words to hold at bay the pain of a failing body, words that commemorate the persistent need to touch, to discover, to survive the loss of assured beauty. Words of water and stone, flesh and desire, reality and imagination, equally fragile, equally enduring–the fossils of our human way.

My Cancer Travels

1

January 15, 1997

I haven't been able to write a word since I was told I have colon cancer. All of it–the bleeding, the tests, the operation, the chemo, the fissure that will not heal, and the doctors who did everything so fast and did not listen to me–all now embody everything I detest, including my own body. Embody. I embody disease and disavowal, blood and shit and a body bound in pain. Everything tastes like acid now, like car batteries in my mouth. If ever words could bring me life, and they have, please please do it now.

A memory: Bayside, Queens, 1952 in the housing development. My twelve-year-old body covered in welts, huge red platelets signifying the body's anger with penicillin. My mother had to go to work. I had pleaded with her to call a doctor, never a child's desire, but we didn't have the money and she didn't have the time. That morning when she saw the welts, she must have known that I needed help. She went to work, but the doctor did come. Did I call the doctor? Did my mother, from the confines of her bookkeeper's office? Have I softened the memory of her neglect? The young doctor came into our disheveled apartment. "Where is your mother? Does she often leave you like this?" he asked as he poured baking powder into the bathtub, helping me lower my tormented body into the cooling bath. "You could have died from this." After the bath, he took me back to my bed and covered the sheets with the same cooling powder. Perhaps he gave me medication to counter my body's anger–I do not remember–but he gave me concern and relief, he gave me care. Another history we have: the history of those who have cared for our bodies.

January 23, 1997

Riverside Park on an early evening in January, the night growing colder by the moment, walking Perry on the adventure I had promised him and me–the curve of the bowl running deep down to the playground–just a shadowy empty town now–the old trees surrounding us. We walk up to the plaza in front of the Civil War Memorial–always a special place for me, the prow of a ship with a tattered flag whipping in the wind, the stone steps leading up to the marble mausoleum, the frozen-in-stone cannonballs passed along the way. I would sit on those steps on summer afternoons with Denver, her big body against me, her shaggy head turned straight ahead–she was the captain of my ship. Always I have adventured in little places, but the glow of freedom, Denver off her leash, Perry running free in the marbled night air, choosing to sit with me, to return to my side–these were wonders. Now, tonight, I give this walk as my gift; for a minute Perry and I are adventurers in the night, the plaza all ours, a lesbian and her dog, a woman with cancer and her dog, the flag of no country straining in the wind, clinking its tether against the masthead of a pole. Soon the cold seeps through my coat, and I turn us toward home. As we walk farther from the park, the night growing darker, I am walking further and further away from all I love.

I hate what is happening to me; I hate the pain, the numbness, the nausea, the cold, the chemo pills waiting for me like small bombs in the Duane Reade bag. I hate it all.

February 25, 1997

"Cancer cells are immortal," said the article in the *New York Times.* "They grow forever in the laboratory." I sit looking at these words. I and so many others are the host to this indomitable life force, a cellular surge to move ahead, leaving us fragile in its wake. Every Tuesday night I go to a Cancer Care support group, my CR group of the '90s, made up of seven women, none of whom are immortal. We come with our bodies scarred by surgeries and treatments, by insertions and removals, we come to tell what the week has brought us; some speak of the small loves they do not want to lose, the warmth of sunlight on a face, the excitement of a trip, the taste of food. We talk of night terrors and the loss of lovers. While the cancer cells inside us glory in their dedication to life, we mark our survival by their death. Doctors call it a war; I do not yet know what to call it, this push and pull between a cell's minute and yet endless passion for life and my own organically larger but perhaps not as determined need to live.

When I lay on the table, a table so thin I thought my large woman's body would hang over the sides, fear shrank my body. I turned my head, taking it all in. The masked doctors, the swiftly moving nurses, the tanks of gases, the light as total as a sun hanging over me. I spoke to myself, about how final all this was and how brave I was to want to take it all in. Do this, Joan, I said. You who have so often thought you needed someone to take care of you, you who gave over so much of yourself to so many over the years, look hard at everything around you. Do not flinch from anything. I turned and saw a palette on which lay scores of scalpels, all nestling into each other, all sharp and shining with the clarity of their purpose. I did not flinch from their sight. If I can look upon the coldness of knives that will slit my skin and not ask anyone to intercede, I will never again betray myself. This is the kind of fem you are, I said to myself, and don't ever forget it.

I have always taken delight in the richness of contradictions, but this one gives no pleasure, no surge of intellectual insight or emotional wisdom. I know I am supposed to be a fighter, a warrior against the intruders, but in these early words, I cannot be. I have always wanted to write hope, to inscribe yearnings—the moments when the face turns to the sun.

2

"I am officially dying," Anita said to me over the phone. The small black box caught the message, but I was lost under the words. I had met Anita in the Cancer Care support group I attended after my own diagnosis and surgery. My last CR group, I thought to myself as I waited with the three other women for our counselor to catch up with us. We met for eight weeks, long enough to know who was dying sooner than the others of us. Anita won the prize. Her breast cancer had metastasized to her brain. She sat, her head wrapped in a dramatic turban, scornfully pointing out to us what novices we were in the cancer journey. A short, edgy woman whose temperament was not improved by her total lack of body hair, her brain-damaged stagger, or her unreturned telephone calls to her doctor, Anita did not court closeness.

Unrepentant optimism did not please Anita either. "Don't give me that 'just a day in the sunshine' bullshit," she would mutter as she carefully picked out the best McDonald's fries from the overflowing grease-stained bag. At the end of her life, Anita developed a passion for junk food. Hamburgers, fries, candy bars. At least I assume this was a newly acquired taste. I knew Anita only at the very end of her life. Because Anita found herself needing a lot of care, very quickly, she had to suffer friends made as quickly as the food she loved to eat. We had immediate intimacy, you could say. I gave a bath to a woman I had not known a month before. I cleaned her kitty box and washed her dishes. I brought my lover over to visit with her, and together we bought her a microwave so her hospice workers could have tea and warmed-up meals. We all had discovered that Anita's stove was as temperamental as she was, blowing up at the mere sight of a match.

Anita Finkel who could barely walk when I met her turned out to be a lover of the ballet and professional ice skating. Anita Finkel turned out to be a New York original. Her apartment was made up of one room and a kitchen. Her bed, the only piece of real furniture in her home, faced a large television screen on which she watched *Jeopardy* the way some people go to church. Every night she was on the phone with a gay male friend guessing the questions, holding on to answers. I too came to know the need for rituals that give the semblance of still being involved with daily life–my choice was *Law and Order.*

But it was on her kitchen table that I found the heart of Anita's life: a computer screen and keyboard and to the side, a neatly stacked series of self-printed dance journals. Everything in Anita's apartment had been subordinated to her love of choreography and movement. Cleanliness, space, possessions, family, perhaps lovers–all had been washed away by her devotion to art. Anita Finkel had made herself into a one-woman school of dance criticism, using all the money she eked out of freelance editorial jobs to publish her dance journal. At her funeral service I learned what a gadfly she had been on the backs of the more conventional dance aficionados, but I had discovered the secret myself when I was making her a cup of tea one afternoon and saw her name on the masthead of the small, square newsletter sitting on her gritty kitchen table.

I was learning about this prima donna on the job. Anita sitting perched up on her bed, growing smaller each day no matter how many calories she consumed, Anita telling me as I stayed arm's length away from her cat, Ariadne, whose talons slashed the air with the same ill temper as her owner's, that she had always been terribly vain about her hair, her small feet, the shoes she compulsively bought–the higher the heels, the better. She exemplified her pride in the past by lifting her leg, now thin and cat-scratched, into the air, clearly expecting me to admire the high arch of her instep. I did, tracing its glory with my finger, while I kept an eye out for the cat. Then the shock of her circumstance would hit her and she would collapse back onto her pillows, her voice growing small with disbelief. "How did this happen to me? I'm too young."

Anita was disdainful of her visitors, methodically turning the pages of the *New York Times*, which she could no longer read, and ignoring their presence until she needed a pill or a glass of water. No longer able to reach for these things without help, she would issue her demand, keeping her head turned away from her provider as her outstretched hand shook in expectation.

The one visitor she looked at full in the face was a small, round woman with dyed red hair, her Portuguese neighbor Maria, who shared what little she had with Anita, who cajoled her into taking baths and changing her nightgown–by the end, Anita's vanity was rhetorical but still in place–who accompanied her to radiation treatments and to the futile cat scans that only verified the loss of brain cells to cancer cells. One day I received a frantic call from Maria. "Joan, we are down at the hospital and Anita has no money and I don't either. We have no car fare to come home." I imagined the two of them, the princess and her gypsy companion, dancing in the streets of some forgotten ballet, trying to flee the cold country of the hospital. I met them at Anita's door and paid the taxi driver. Maria, whom no one thanked at the funeral service, made sure that Anita had something to eat every day. I promised her the microwave "when it was all over," as I euphemistically put it, but one of Anita's fellow dance critics got to it first.

At her memorial service, where I met the public Anita for the first time, I learned that in her closing days she had selected the part of the Bible with which she could live–the Book of Psalms. In the late hours of the night she asked the visiting rabbi to chant their words of adoration and anger, a mixture of beauty and sternness that I can only imagine approached her own aesthetic.

Because of my own cancer, I became part of Anita's dying. And in her dying I learned about her life, a New York life lived in a rent-controlled apartment, filled with an acid-laced dream of swooping grace. She did not approve of her death. "This should not have happened. How did this happen? I am too young," she said to me over and over on the phone until the last time, when half her words were gibberish, and she did not know it.

Behold you are beautiful, my love;
Behold, you are beautiful.

3

She stands, so fresh and open, in the doorway, a gray scarf hung loosely from her muscled neck. Her green winter jacket is already zipped, and in her right hand is a large blue carry-all, bulging with tools. I turn to say good-bye and all time stops. This woman with whom I have shared a decade as lovers. This woman who on her fiftieth birthday ran with dogs over a Maine lake turned to ice, who had slept on spruce boughs with the snow under her, this woman who loved the feel of wood and glass, bending them into shapes to hold the earth, to catch the light, this woman who walked with poets, holding close to the words of May Swenson, saying them into my sleep so I could see how they spun with meaning.

This woman who sat by my bed in a darkened hospital room, hour after hour, keeping guard. One night in the hazy but impenetrable sleep of drugs, I felt someone tug at my fingers and thought it was the nurse taking my blood, but it was my love gently sliding back onto my finger the ring she had given me ten years ago, before the flood of cells.

This woman who would take me in her arms, lift my whole body up, and settle me back down on a nest of pillows, preparing me for love. This woman who would lower herself on top of me, her weight so good, so full of promise. I held her to me, my fingers gripping her back, so solid with her strength, so hard with her passionate determination to give pleasure, to force desire into sound. Once in the beginning, on a mattress on the floor of her Brooklyn apartment, we made love for eighteen hours. Every time I said there is no more, she proved me wrong. She bought me a rhinestone pin shaped as the number 18, so when I was speaking or reading in a public place, I would remember that private time.

This woman who worked with my words and images of lesbian history, filling a red notebook with the choreography of my presentation, so word and pictured face would carry meaning, who ran me through my lines night after night when I was to play a St. Louis madam in a lesbian play down on Fourth Street, who sat in the darkened theater, performance after performance, trying to will me into remembering.

This woman who worked tirelessly to serve the community she loved, coming home after longer and longer days and nights at endless meetings, fighting for a sick man's apartment or for a public place we could call home or to educate the police into holding back their hatred or the teachers into talking about us as if we had a history, who hung on the walls of a city office building the first pictured history of our community, this woman who walked away when asked to leave, defeated by a political shift that did not care about her excellence, this woman who wrote a book between physical calamities and worries about a job, who never let go of the possibility of a task completed if she had anything to do with it, this woman who won Mabel's love with her Kansas ways and Friday-night dinners, the table all shiny with candlelight. "Where did you find this one?" Mabel would ask me, winking in the shadows. "You better hold on to her!"

This woman who wondered where my passion went, and waited while I wrote and talked of love, waited for my body to return, and cried with pain, with me, for what had seeped away in the hospital night, in the childhood years.

This woman who tirelessly moved earth and stone, shaping Catskill hardness into Catskill meadow, who sought adventure with a child's delight, who loves the beauty of a woman all in color, this woman who in all her wonders and her gifts laughs in the face of those who say we are less than life, this woman who stayed and stayed and tried and tried to hold on to me, to us, is at the door. I turn to say good-bye, and all time stops.

4

In February of 1998–a year after my surgery–I was asked to participate in a reading from a new collection of lesbian erotica edited by Karen Tulchinsky, a good sturdy friend from Vancouver, Canada. She had selected my story "A Different Place," a story written in 1986 that celebrated the pleasure of anal fucking. This was my first public appearance as a writer since the cancer, and up to the last minute I did not know if I would be able to read that story in public. Everyone before me read from their piece that appeared in the collection. When I stepped up to the microphone, I thought I would give it a try, but as I read the opening passages of the story, describing the preparation Jay was going through to be ready to perform anal penetration, I knew that I would stop before the scene of entry. I have colon-rectal cancer and it may kill me; that story overwhelmed the narrative of a night of pleasure in Connecticut over ten years ago. Torn between still wanting to preserve the space I had opened for my audience, the space that allowed women to enjoy all forms of sexual activity, and my own recent need for sexual silence, I chose as gracefully as I could to leave them with the sense of wonderful expectation, the promise that the story would bring them pleasure–but I could not go there with them, I explained, because of my cancer.

This writing about the queer body, this revealing of open thighs and scratched backs, this wet hard use of language is not always an easy thing to do. This mapping of where hands push in, of where mouths suck out, this capturing of sex sounds, of murmurs and moans, of shouts and cries, of yes and more and now and now and please don't stop is not always welcomed in this world. And because the heart follows the mouth and the hand, when I am on my knees before my lover, cupping her ass with my spread fingers, pushing her cock forward into my mouth, my breasts swelling with the weight of all her wonder, I am always surprised by the anger awaiting these words. But something pushes at me to keep finding words for the bend of the back, the thrust of the fist, the woman's cock in my woman's mouth, the taste of her cunt, my breast covered with the wetness of want, legs spread so far apart that countries could enter. And so I wrote of these things, as a fem woman, as a woman who has lain on her back and pushed at her lover's hand for more, who has helped buckle the leather straps of her lover's harness so desire could shape the air.

My friend John Preston read my words. From long distances over years, he kept a lookout for the assaults; postcards would arrive after some public battle, just a sentence from one pornographer to another. Be strong, my friend, he said. Later, when we spent more time together, I learned as he spoke in his raspy, tired voice that he too was always saying thank you, thank you to the middle-aged salesman who had taken a young man to his hotel room one night and after the stroking and sucking, as their bodies cooled down, had told him never betray your own voice.

It is not easy to open the body to words, to make a life of sex writing. Comrades are needed, friends who understand both the bravado and the yearning, friends who know that even if all your skill is poured into the portrait of the ass raised for entry, you will never be called a writer. Preston, as he signed his letters, stood so tall; he was to me so gallant; he knew that a woman writing about sex was different from a man; but he always wanted more, more challenges to the silences imposed on the body.

My dear pornographer, we had planned so much together, collaborations of erotic wanderings fiercely anchored in clear direct seeable language. Now you have traveled ahead; your words of comfort are pieces of a treasure. When once again the body calls for its own language, for its own image of desire, I write sex for John.

    This is now my battle: to win back from the specifics of medical treatment—from the outrage of an invaded body where hands I did not know touched parts of myself that I will never see—my own body, my own body so marked by the hands and lips of lovers, now so lonely in its fear. Touch my scar, knead my belly, don't be afraid of my cancer. Enter me the old way, not through the skin cut open, but because I am calling to you through the movement of my hips, the breath that pleads for your hand to touch the want of me. Heal me because you do not fear me, touch me because you do not fear the future. Cancer and sex. One I have and one I must have.

5

    Like a little girl bringing out a favorite doll, I shouted from the bedroom, "I need to show you something." You, my new friend, were sitting at the dining-room table and turned expectantly toward me when I reappeared. "I need you to see this," I said, holding up my shirt and pulling down the band of my pants so you could see the still-red scar that started at my waist, skirted my belly button, and made its way down to the beginning of my pubic triangle.

    I stood in front of you, not clear about why I was doing this, a fifty-seven-year-old woman exhibiting her cancer scar to a new friend. You reached out and traced the path of the incision with your fingers, and I started to cry. Not a little girl anymore, but a woman with colon cancer, a cancer that should have been found when I had the colonoscopy done a year before the tumor grew so large it invaded the surrounding tissue, but that a rushed doctor had missed. "I pulled out too quickly," he told me later, after the tumor had broken through the wall of my colon and spilled red blood into the toilet bowl. "Have you cried yet?" he asked me in 1997. It took a year for the tears to come, and they came only when I stood in front of a woman whom I wanted to touch me, to make love to me like it used to be.

It will never be like it used to be. Cancer has claimed me; "my cancer," I say now, like others talk about their cars or children. We suggest you have a year of chemo, the doctors said, and I did—or as much of it as I could stand. For that whole year, I did not allow anyone to touch me, except doctors, nurses, technicians. My body was filled with chemicals that sickened me. I sat on the edges of tables in small cubicles, the IV needle precariously housed in my arm, in a small vein on the back of my hand, or anywhere else the oncologist could find a vein large enough and strong enough to absorb the needle and the acid. Sometimes the vein would collapse, and the chemo would start pouring out under my skin. "You are lucky," the doctor said. "This chemo is not as dangerous as some of the others."

And I knew he was right. I was one of the "lucky" ones. I would keep my hair; I avoided a shunt; I only had 500 mg of 5-FU every week with 50 mg of Leucovorin, a form of Folic acid, a natural substance that some people want to ingest. I had not been able to take the initial treatment, 5-FU with Ergamisole, a drug used to kill worms in the stomachs of sheep. After two treatments with the little white pills, I did not care if I lived or died.

This is not the story of every cancer patient; it is my own, just like this cancer, this colon-rectal cancer, is my own. Just like this body, now a year and a half after the surgeon removed four feet of colon, my transverse colon, and reattached my intestines in a new configuration, is my own. I need you to know all the details, the scientific names, the side effects, just as I had to learn them. Illness, like sex, gives the body another dimension, makes it transparent. I could feel the chemotherapy liquid enter my veins, trace its burning journey through my arm, just as I used to feel a lover's tongue trail down my neck.

6

Ten years have passed since I crossed the seas. Ten years of work and play and then so much loss. Now I hold the renewed passport in my hand. All because of you, because you insist on hope, a hope that sings in your upturned phrases, that sits perched on your backpack sharing its bumpy ride down the streets of Havana, London, Melbourne, New York, Beijing. You make a home in whatever city your work takes you, your true home being the ideas that shape your vision of a world more equitable in its securities while still thriving with difference.

Wherever there is a desk, you live. I have watched you work, my black slippery coat with its gold dragon draped around your shoulders, books and papers piled around you as, hour after hour, you read through texts, always looking for the insight that will move your work along, that will push into place the next step of your argument. The huge shadows of your antagonists hover over you, the governments and the banks, the soldiers and the courts all pitted against the fall of your red hair, the squareness of your copied words. I turn to look again as I go back into my room to put my own words on paper, and see the frail strength of the future, your comrades, like yourself, working in so many places in the world, trying to chip away at the stolid face of unquestioned, unquestioning power.

I am afraid to leave what I know, to leave my home. I am afraid to take my body with its fumbles and mysteries into countries where I have never lived. And then you lay me down, and laugh gently in my ear. "You're a funny old thing," you say. I cling to you, to the difference of you, your sounds and smells from so far away, too far away. I weep into your shoulder. "I'll be back," you always say before leaving.

But now you are here, your hand moving down my belly, your hair trailing its red fingers over my face. I tense with waiting for the homecoming, and then you reach me and pause before my hunger. This is another kind of power, one that leaps from your hand into my heart. You pull your head back so you can watch how I will take you in, how I will arch with pleasure, my head thrown back with the wonder of the first thrust, and then all my will sinks to my hips and I call to you to never stop, to keep entering me with your difference, with the worlds you carry on your fingertips, to paint my caves red with your travels.

I hadn't thought it possible or wanted it. The night before you were to leave for England, the day we heard the news that Marjorie had died her cancer death, we made love as if all the days and nights ahead of us were lost in darkness.

You were lying against the pillows, your red hair spreading across them, your lipstick making the blue of your eyes even sharper. I get caught on those eyes; I think I see in them the seas I will never see–the endless blue on the map surrounding the continent of Australia, a blue I fear because it is as vast and unknown as death itself. You turned toward me when I entered, your body urging me to hurry. "I want you," you said as I bent over you, taking you in my arms. I was deeply moved by your direct request and by my knowledge that I could meet your need.

I kissed hard and then light, kissed your neck and shoulders and throat. I wetted your nipples, my mouth pulling on them through the sheen of your nightgown. I buried my head in your hair, pushing your face to one side with my cheek. I just wanted to touch you, to taste you, to make up for years of fear, of deprivation. Your breasts swelled to my mouth and I pulled them free of the gown, rounding them in my hands, resting my head against their swell. Here was an ocean I could survive.

I slowly caressed the wetness out from between your drawn-up legs, opening you up, making love to every fold and crevice of your sex, knowing just what I was doing, and letting you know that I held your need in my hand. I was making love as much to your belief in me as to your body.

I leaned over you so my mouth could pleasure you, and I could see so clearly the movements of my fingers, the redness of your cunt, taking me in. I entered you, pushing against the swollen flesh until it gave way; then slowly, I moved in and out while I sucked you into my mouth, all of you bursting in my mouth like all things hot and moist and deep. You were all around me, your thighs like high walls keeping me in, your breasts above me still hard with want, your sounds, small moans, sharp intakes of breath and I was in all of you. You came in the way I had come to know, first small gripping of orgasms, and then as I kept on, not fooled by these first signs of pleasure, you pulled up into yourself, your moans becoming a hot wind above me, and roared your full giving into my mouth, on my fingers, through my soul.

Then your broad shoulders rose into the night, and your face looking down at me became my total vista. You smiled as you untied my black silk jacket. I asked you to turn the light off, and a sadness flickered across your face. "I will, darling, if you want me to." You leaned across me and the room fell into darkness. Now I could allow all to happen.

You kissed me deep and full, the kiss I had such a hard time accepting when we first started to explore our desire. Like the whore I sometimes was, kissing was the gift I did not give away. After such a drought, I was afraid of the intimacy of kissing, not of fucking, but of the hungry touch of mouths. One day in Riverside Park, with the sun falling into the river, you had held my head so I could not turn it away and forced me to take kiss, your tongue. Now I raised my head in hungry pursuit of your lips, wanting more and more of you.

Your large, strong body, the assurance with which you maneuvered me under you—you surprised me. This woman, who was so languid an hour before, who half-draped her eyes with receptive want, now bent over me, holding me, teasing my nipples until I moaned for relief. I could feel your smile moving over my body as you spread my legs with your knee. "You keep open for me," you said, and I did not move. I felt you reach for the small bottle of lubricant we kept near the pillow. You kneeled between my legs, bathing your hand in the slippery lotion, your shadow large against the moonlight. Suddenly, very quickly, before I could contract with resistance, I felt your hugeness enter me. Your hand, sleek in its liquid coating, pushed past the guarding muscles, and you had me, all of me, waiting on your smallest move, longing for your thrusts. Not even breathing was as important as your next motion. "This is what you will remember each day I am away," you whispered, forcing the turn of my head by your grip on my hair. And you thrust into me with such power that my whole body moved into the air, "and this," you said again and again. Five times you took me with your hand, five times, one for each day you would be away. Then you stopped and I trembled in your arms, and you lifted me, held me, against you. I was emptied, or so I thought.

We lay in the darkness, my head on your shoulder, waiting for calmer breaths, the air still heavy with our need. You asked me to enter you. I did. And then you entered me, not all of you, not like what had come before, but enough so my swollen clit could feel you, and then you said, "Now fuck me," and I started to move my fingers in you. With all my focus on you, I did not realize for the first few seconds that you, too, were moving inside me, on me, that our bodies were moving together, pushing toward the same pleasure. This was something I would never have allowed, this sameness of penetration, this blurring of bodies, and you had known that. Before I could take in what was happening, I was coming in bursting waves upon you, and you, pushed by my movements, came with me.

Too exhausted to move, too amazed at what had happened, I just lay alongside of you. "You see, Joan," you said, your Australian accent incongruously crisp in the sex-scented night air, "it is all possible for me, for us, all of it."

7

Ten days had passed, ten nights of late-night telephone calls to her Havana hotel, just to hear her voice. Sometimes she would take the telephone out to the balcony–so I could hear the ocean, she would say. I pictured her, standing in her nightgown, the dark, warm night lifting the gown's edges, her breasts outlined by the wind. Ringlets of hair weighed down with the wetness of the night. The sounds of that ocean never did reach me, but I knew what I was supposed to hear, and I could see in the darkness of my room, the white heads rolling onto the beach, the curving sea wall that enclosed the people suffering in their beautiful city, suffering from the vindictiveness of my own government.

She told me, as I yearned for her, that at dusk young lovers drape themselves over the sea wall, their bodies hard with want. In all the cities of the world torn by war or hatred, crumbling from bullets or embargoes, citizens search for the alley or rooftop that will harbor their love. I want the governments to know this, to know that this century is marked by people's struggle to survive the deadliness of officials, young men and women, the lovers, proclaiming their hope in the grips of flesh.

Havana, all torn by history and hope, was home to my lover, and I was jealous of its hold on her. My own history was crumbling and I, too, wanted my love to hold back the emptiness of disaster. But countries are larger than hearts, and so the days passed, and I did my days.

The night of her return was marked by hours of delay, connections missed, planes delayed, hours added to hours until late into the night. Finally I heard her push the door open, heard the roll of her suitcase and her voice calling out, "Darling, I'm home."

I carefully walked out of my bedroom into the hallway and saw her there. Brown and red from the sun, her throat bare, her eyes wide with excitement. I could barely see her for the brightness of the sun she carried with her that late night. We held each other for long long moments, my head buried in her neck. I could smell her travels, taste the distance that had stretched out between us. She held me firmly in her arms, her blouse rolled up so her forearms were bare, and I thought in how so short a time I had come to know the path of her veins, the lie of the muscles beneath her soft skin. She held me and held me, my need of her part of the history she had seen.

8

"My dear, my dear it is not so dreadful here"*

Late at night, when even the raw sounds of the city drift farther away, I sit alone, listening once again to the story of my body. No lover's hands will keep me from my self. Lee sleeps downtown, wrapped in the arms of her new lover; Dianne has flown back over the oceans to her vast continent of friends and work. I stare at the wall in front of me. Like so many others, I am caught in the limbo of cancer, the still place at the heart of the night. I cannot travel back to the physical safety I once thought I had, and I can't go forward with any assurances that I have a future. I am not unique in this stasis, but this is my bedroom, my history; these are my questions of endurance. How will I travel in my life? What belongings will I carry with me?

Let my desire remain, even if the cancer grows again into its gray mounds of life. Let my breasts and cunt grow hard with answering determination. And let me keep what I have learned from this illness–that terror is a human thing, that the body, even in its vomit and blood, wants to stand on its feet again, that kindness makes its way through the dead skin, that sickness too yearns for its human voice.

These are my travels. Late in the night, I will go deep into my body's story and hear its tale of life battling life. And as I welcomed home my other beloved travelers, I will bury my head in the gift of hope only I can bring to the surface.

A line from a poem by Edna St. Vincent Millay, written to mourn the death of a young willful woman lover. The poet asks Persephone to comfort her frightened friend who wanders weeping like a lost child in the wilds of Hades. I thank Naomi Replansky, my friend who is also a poet, for bringing me these words.

The Price of Memory

*Miss Meagher said the problem of wandering bison
began in the mid '70s when the herd leaders discovered the rich winter habitat along the river outside the park. Now, she said, the most feasible way
to keep the bison in the park may be to shoot the
animals that know about the rich grasses outside.
"What we need is to remove the knowledge by
removing the animals."*
– *New York Times,* November 10, 1985. The story
was accompanied by a picture of a dying bison
lying in the snow after having been shot by one of
the keepers of the herd.

Large bowed heads, nostrils wide with life,
Two times the floods have come to drown your
     greenly growing grasses
Once when you were free with dust and clouds of
breath, and ran with steaming dung beneath
     your feet,

You moved in your own time with no fear of memory
Until the bullets sang.
Then heads and tails became dead things.
Once before you were the hunted ones,
Until your stars, hung with skulls, fell from the skies.

A few of you kept captive on protected lands
grew slowly into memory,
and then the words came,
kill those who remember.

Your eyes are dull,
snow reddens from your bloodied hair
lying under your heavy head like a sleeping lover

Sleep now memory
horns tipped with black, pointing back to safer lands

Three young men stand a small way off,
smiling at their kill.
Even standing they breathe less life than you.

You carried secret sweetnesses
in your massive skulls
Breathed out your memories in clouds of warmed air.
What did we fear so much that only bullets could be found?
Was it your smell, your sound, your numbers?
Was it your audacity to find what you needed to live?

Before they fall, the hunted ones call out their history,
The grasses live, the grasses live
there beyond the place we have been given.

Tell the calves, the awkward frisky ones,
whisper into their small ears,
This dry dust is not all there is.

Tell this tale of greenness
which earned the brave ones death,
for without this dream of hope, we cannot live.

Joan Nestle:
A Bibliography

Books

A Fragile Union: New and Collected Writings (1987–1998). San Francisco: Cleis Press, 1998.

The Persistent Desire: A Femme-Butch Reader. Boston: Alyson, 1992.

A Restricted Country. Ithaca: Firebrand Books, 1987. Reprinted, London, Pandora Press: 1996.

Sister and Brother: Lesbians and Gay Men Write About Their Lives Together, edited with John Preston. San Francisco: HarperSanFrancisco, 1994.

Women on Women: An Anthology of Lesbian Short Fiction, edited with Naomi Holoch. New York: New American Library, 1990.

Women on Women 2: An Anthology of Lesbian Short Fiction, edited with Naomi Holoch. New York: Plume, 1993.

Women on Women 3: An Anthology of Lesbian Short Fiction, edited with Naomi Holoch. New York: Plume, 1996.

Worlds Unspoken: An Anthology of International Lesbian Fiction, edited with Naomi Holoch. New York: Vintage, 1999.

Essays, Stories, and Poems

"Afterword." In *Creating a Place for Ourselves: Lesbian, Gay, and Bisexual Community Histories*, edited by Brett Beemyn. New York: Routledge, 1997.

"The Bathroom Line." *Gay Community News* (October 4, 1980). Reprinted in *Lesbian Connection*, September, 1981.

"Beaches and Bars: Places of Restriction and Reclamation." In *Queers in Space: Communities, Public Places, Sites of Resistance*, edited by Gordon Brent Ingram, Anne-Marie Bouthillette, and Yolanda Retter. Seattle: Bay Press, 1997.

"Butch-Fem Relationships: Sexual Courage in the Fifties." *Heresies 12* (May 1981). Reprinted in *Body Politic*, 1981; *Sapphic Touch*, 1981 *Emma*, 1982 (German), *Diva*, 1982 (Dutch), *Sexualidat* 1982/3 (German).

"A Change of Life." *Bad Attitude* (Winter 1985). Reprinted in *Diva*, 1985 (Dutch).

"Desire Perfected: Lesbian Sex After Forty." In *Lesbians at Midlife: The Creative Transition*, edited by Barbara Sang, Joyce Warshow, and Adrienne J. Smith. San Francisco: Spinsters Ink, 1990.

"Early Words on Living with Cancer." *New York City Lesbian Health Fair Journal*, May 3, 1997: 13–17.

"Esther's Story." *B.A.D. News*, August, 1981. Reprinted in *Penguin Book of Lesbian Short Stories*, edited by Margaret Reynolds. New York: Penguin, 1994 and in *An Intimate Wilderness: Lesbian Writers on Sexuality*, ed. Judith Barrington. Portland, Oregon: Eighth Mountain Press, 1991.

"A Feeling Comes." *Homologie*, June 1988 (Dutch). Reprinted in *Lesbian Love Stories*, vol. 2, edited by Irene Zahava. Freedom, CA: The Crossing Press, 1989.

"The Fem Question: We Will Not Go Away." In *Pleasure and Danger: Exploring Female Sexuality*, ed. Carole S. Vance. Boston: Routledge, 1984. Reprinted as "Nosotras que nos queremos tanto...," *Revista Feminista*, no. 6, February 1988 (Spanish) and in *We Are Everywhere*, edited by Mark Blasius and Shane Phelan. New York: Routledge, 1997.

"A Fem's Feminist History." In *Live, from Feminism: Memoirs of Women's Liberation*, edited by Rachel Blau DuPlessis and Ann Snitow. New York: Crown Books, 1998.

"Foreword." In *Eye to Eye: Portraits of Lesbians*, Joan E.

Biren. Washington, DC: Glad Hag Books, 1979.

"The Gift of Taking." *On Our Backs* (Winter 1984). Reprinted in *Diva Lesbisch*, July 1985 (Dutch).

"Homophobia and Private Courage." Essay in the catalog for the City Hall exhibit, "Prejudice and Pride: The NYC Lesbian and Gay Community, World War II to the Present, June, 1988."

"Hope." *Bad Attitude* (Summer 1987).

"I Lift My Eyes to the Hill: The Life of Mabel Hampton as Told by a White Woman." In *Queer Representations: Reading Lives, Reading Cultures*, edited by Martin Duberman. New York: NYU Press, 1997.

"Introduction." *Common Lives/Lesbian Lives* 12 (1984).

"I Wanted to Live Long Enough to Kiss a Woman: The Life of Lesbian Literature," introduction to *Photographic Archives of Gay and Lesbian Writers*, by Robert Giraud. Cambridge: M.I.T. Press, 1997.

"Lesbian Memories 1: Riis Park, 1960," *Common Lives/Lesbian Lives* (June 1983).

"Lesbians," "Lesbian Herstory Archives," "African American Women United for Social Change." Entries (with Lee Hudson) in *Encyclopedia of New York City*, edited by Kenneth T. Jackson. New York: Yale University Press, 1995.

"Lesbians and Prostitutes: An Historical Sisterhood." In *Sex Work: Writings by Women in the Sex Industry*, edited by Frédérique Delacoste and Priscilla Alexander. San Francisco: Cleis Press, 1987, 1998. Reprinted *in Good Girls/Bad Girls: Feminists and Sex Trade Workers, Face to Face*. edited by Laurie Bell, Seattle: Seal Press, 1987.

"Liberties Not Taken." *B.A.D. News* (January 1982).

"Living with Herstory." *Lesbian Insider, Insighter, Inciter* (March 1983). Reprinted in *Body Politic*, September 1983 (Canada). Keynote Address presented at Amazon Autumn Sixth Annual Conference, November, 1982.

"Many Days of Courage." 20th Anniversary gay pride rally in Central Park on June 24, 1989, *OutWeek* 3 (July 10, 1998): 28.

"Marcia's Room." *Focus* (March–April 1980).

"Margaret." *Bad Attitude* (Summer 1987).

"My History with Censorship." *Bad Attitude* (Spring 1985).

Reprinted in *Slechte Meiden* Nr 5, 1986 (Dutch).

"My Mother Liked to Fuck." *Womannews*, December–January, 1981–2. Reprinted in *The Eight Technologies of Otherness*, edited by Sue Golding. London: Routledge, 1997 and *Powers of Desire: The Politics of Sexuality*. edited by Ann Snitow and Christine Stansell. New York: Monthly Review Press, 1983.

"An Old Story." In *Lesbian Path*, edited by M. Cruikshank. Grey Fox Press, 1985.

"Oral History with Gabi." In *Lesbiot: Israeli Lesbians Talk About Sexuality, Feminism, Judaism and Their Lives*, edited by Tracy Moore. London: Cassell, 1994.

"Our Gift of Touch." *Conditions* 17 (1990).

"Preface: In the Beginning." In *The Lesbian Periodicals Index* by Clare Potter (with Deborah Edel). Tallahasee: Naiad Press, 1986.

"Proud to Be Passionate: Lesbian Sex and Censorship." In *Pride Guide '85* (June 1985): 25–26.

"Radical Archiving from a Lesbian Feminist Perspective." *Gay Insurgent* (Spring 1979).

"A Restricted Country." *Sinister Wisdom* (Summer 1982).

"Stone Butch, Drag Butch, Baby Butch." *B.A.D. News* (August 1981).

"A Sturdy Yes of a People: An Open Letter to My Community." *Gay Community News*, June 1993.

"This Illness Is No Figment of Our Imaginations." *Gay Community News* 16 (May 21–27, 1989): 12ff.

"The Three." *On Our Backs* (Spring 1986).

"Two Women of Difference." *13th Moon* (September 1983).

"Two Women: Regina Nestle, 1910-1978, and Her Daughter, Joan." In *Every Woman I've Ever Loved: Lesbian Writers on Their Mothers*, edited by Catherine Reid and Holly Iglesias. San Francisco: Cleis Press, 1997.

"The Uses of Strength." In *Heatwave: Women in Love and Lust*, edited by Lucy Jane Bledsoe. Los Angeles: Alyson Press, 1995.

"Wet Words." *Bad Attitude*, Winter, 1985. Reprinted *in Wanting Women: An Anthology of Erotic Lesbian Poetry*, edited by Jan Hardy. Pittsburgh: Sidewalk Revolution Press, 1990.

"Woman Poppa." *On Our Backs*, 1988. Reprinted in *Lesbian Love Stories*, edited by Irene Zahava. Freedom, CA: The Crossing Press, 1989.

"Woman of Muscle, Woman of Bone." *Bad Attitude*, No. 6, 1990. Reprinted in *Tangled Sheets: Stories and Poems of Lesbian Lust*, edited by Rosamund Elwin and Karen X. Tulchinsky. Toronto: Women's Press, 1995.

"Writing Sex for John." In *Looking for Mr. Preston: A Celebration of the Writer's Life*, edited by Laura Antoniou. New York: Masquerade Books, 1995.

Interviews

"A Fem's Own Story," with Margaret Hunt. *Gay Community News* (October 4–10, 1987): 16ff.

"I'll Be the Girl: Generations of Fem," with Barbara Cruikshank. In *Femme: Feminists, Lesbians and Bad Girls*, eds. Laura Harris and Elizabeth Crocker. New York: Routledge, 1997.

"Interview with Joan Nestle," with Holly Metz. *American Voices* (Winter 1990): 73–84.

"Joan Nestle: Keep Flaunting It," with Lissette Chang. *Womannews* (June 1990), 1ff.

"Lesbian Writer Fights Feminist Censors," with Holly Metz. *The Progressive* (August 1989): 16.

"Our Favorite Femme," with Sue George. *Square Peg* (1988): 10–11.

"Pleasure, Guilt and Other Slippery Territory," with Robin Podolsky. *Forward Motion* (September 1989): 56–62.

"Queen Mother: Archivist Joan Nestle Is a Voice Against Forgetting," with Liz Galst. *The Worcester Phoenix* (May 13, 1994): 8–9.

"Stonewall: A Gift to the World. An Interview with Joan Nestle and Tony Kushner." *Found Object* 4 (Fall 1994): 94–107.

"Taking Pride in Lesbian Herstory," with Susie Day. *Sojourner* 14 (June 1989): 17–19.

Untitled, *Feminist Collections*, 1981

Untitled, *Sinister Wisdom*, 1979

"We Are All Part of This Circle of Difference: An Interview with Joan Nestle," with Isa Leshko. *Sojourner* 20 (June 1995): 9ff.

Articles About Joan Nestle

Hogan, Steve, and Lee Hudson. "Joan Nestle." In *Completely Queer: The Gay and Lesbian Encyclopedia*. New York: Henry Holt, 1998.

"Joan Nestle." In *The Oxford Companion to Women's Writing in the United States*. Cathy Davidson and Linda Wagner-Martin, eds. New York: Oxford University Press, 1995.

Martindale, Kathleen. "Toward a Butch-Femme Reading Practice: Reading Joan Nestle." In *Un/popular Culture: Lesbian Writing After the Sex Wars*. Albany: SUNY Pess, 1997.

Rochman, Susan. "Joan Nestle." In *Contemporary Lesbian Writers of the United States. A Bio-Bibliographical Critical Sourcebook*, edited by Sandra Pollack and Denise D. Knight. Westport, CT: Greenwood Press, 1993.

Stanley, Deborah. "Joan Nestle." In *Gay and Lesbian Literature*, edited by Wayne R. Dynes, Barbara G. Grier, Sharon Malinowski. Detroit: St. James Press, 1994.

Szymczak, Jerome. "Joan Nestle: American Archivist and Writer." In *Outstanding Lives: Profiles of Lesbians and Gay Men*, edited by Michael Bronski, Christa Brelin, and Michael J. Tyrkus. New York: Visible Ink Press, 1997.

Whatling, Claire. "Reading Awry: Joan Nestle and the Recontextualization of Heterosexuality." In *Sexual Sameness: Textual Differences in Lesbian and Gay Writing*, edited by Joseph Bristow, 1992.

Film and Video

Just Because of Who We Are, a documentary on anti-lesbian violence. Produced by Heramedia, 1988.

Lesbian Voices: Currents. PBS, June 1988.

Neighborhood Voices: Greenwich Village. WNYC Foundation. Produced by B. Kerr and Amber Hollibaugh, 1986.

About the Author

Joan Nestle was born in New York City in 1940, a working class Jew raised by her mother who worked as a bookkeeper in the garment industry. She came out as lesbian in Greenwich Village in the 1950s, marched in Selma in 1965, joined the ranks of the feminist movement in 1971, and helped establish the Gay Academic Union in 1972. In 1973, Nestle co-founded the Lesbian Herstory Archives, which now fills a three-story building in Park Slope, Brooklyn. Joan Nestle is the author *of A Restricted Country* and editor *of The Persistent Desire: A Femme-Butch Reader.* She is co-editor (with Naomi Holoch) of *Worlds Unspoken: An Anthology of International Lesbian Fiction* and the *Women on Women* lesbian fiction series. With John Preston, she co-edited *Sister and Brother: Lesbians and Gay Men Write About Their Lives Together.* She has won numerous awards, including the Bill Whitehead Award for Lifetime Achievement in Lesbian and Gay Literature, America Library Association Gay/Lesbian Book Award and the Lambda Literary Award for Lesbian Nonfiction. She lives in New York.

Books from Cleis Press

Sexual Politics

Forbidden Passages: Writings Banned in Canada, introductions by Pat Califia and Janine Fuller. Lambda Literary Award Winner. ISBN: 1-57344-019-1 14.95 paper.

Public Sex: The Culture of Radical Sex by Pat Califia. ISBN: 0-939416-89-1 12.95 paper.

Real Live Nude Girl: Chronicles of Sex-Positive Culture by Carol Queen. ISBN: 1-57344-073-6. 14.95 paper.

Sex Work: Writings by Women in the Sex Industry, second edition, edited by Frédérique Delacoste and Priscilla Alexander. ISBN: 1-57344-042-6. 19.95 paper.

Susie Bright's Sexual Reality: A Virtual Sex World Reader by Susie Bright. ISBN: 0-939416-59-X 9.95 paper.

Susie Bright's Sexwise by Susie Bright. ISBN: 1-57344-002-7 10.95 paper.

Susie Sexpert's Lesbian Sex World, second edition, by Susie Bright.ISBN: 1-57344-077-9. 14.95 paper.

Gender Transgression

Body Alchemy: Transsexual Portraits by Loren Cameron. Lambda Literary Award Winner. ISBN: 1-57344-062-0 24.95 paper.

Dagger: On Butch Women, edited by Roxxie, Lily Burana, Linnea Due. ISBN: 0-939416-82-4 14.95 paper.

I Am My Own Woman: The Outlaw Life of Charlotte von Mahlsdorf, translated by Jean Hollander. ISBN: 1-57344-010-8 12.95 paper.

PoMoSexuals: Challenging Assumptions about Gender and Sexuality edited by Carol Queen and Lawrence Schimel. Preface by Kate Bornstein. ISBN: 1-57344-074-4 14.95 paper.

Sex Changes: The Politics of Transgenderism by Pat Califia ISBN: 1-57344-072-8 16.95 paper.

Switch Hitters: Lesbians Write Gay Male Erotica and Gay Men Write Lesbian Erotica, edited by Carol Queen and Lawrence Schimel. ISBN: 1-57344-021-3 12.95 paper.

Lesbian and Gay Studies

The Case of the Good-For-Nothing Girlfriend, second edition, by Mabel Maney. Lambda Literary Award Nominee. ISBN: 1-57344-075-2 16.95 paper.

The Case of the Not-So-Nice Nurse by Mabel Maney. Lambda Literary Award Nominee. ISBN: 0-939416-76-X 9.95 paper.

Chasing the American Dyke Dream: Homestrectch edited by Susan Fox Rogers. ISBN: 1-57344-036-1 $14.95 paper.

Nancy Clue and the Hardly Boys in *A Ghost in the Closet* by Mabel Maney. Lambda Literary Award Nominee. ISBN: 1-57344-012-4 10.95 paper.

Different Daughters: A Book by Mothers of Lesbians, second edition, edited by Louise Rafkin. ISBN: 1-57344-050-7 12.95 paper.

A Lesbian Love Advisor by Celeste West. ISBN: 0-939416-26-3 9.95 paper.

On the Rails: A Memoir, second edition, by Linda Niemann. Introduction by Leslie Marmon Silko. ISBN: 1-57344-064-7. 14.95 paper.

Debut Literature
The Little School: Tales of Disappearance and Survival , second edition, by Alicia Partnoy. ISBN: 1-57344-029-9 14.95 paper.

Marianne Faithfull's Cigarette: Poems by Gerry Gomez Pearlberg. ISBN: 1-57344-034-5 $12.95 paper

Memory Mambo by Achy Obejas. Lambda Literary Award Winner. ISBN: 1-57344-017-5 12.95 paper.

Queer Dog: Homo Pup Poetry, edited by Gerry Gomez Pearlberg. ISBN: 1-57344-071-X. 12.95. paper.

We Came All The Way from Cuba So You Could Dress Like This?: Stories by Achy Obejas. Lambda Literary Award Nominee. ISBN: 0-939416-93-X 10.95 paper.

Seeing Dell by Carol Guess ISBN: 1-57344-023-X 12.95 paper.

Mysteries
Dirty Weekend: A Novel of Revenge by Helen Zahavi. ISBN: 0-939416-85-9 10.95 paper.

The Woman Who Knew Too Much: A Cordelia Morgan Mystery by B. Reese Johnson. ISBN: 1-57344-045-0. 12.95 paper.

Vampires & Horror
Brothers of the Night: Gay Vampire Stories edited by Michael Rowe and Thomas S. Roche. ISBN: 1-57344-025-6 14.95 paper.

Dark Angels: Lesbian Vampire Stories, edited by Pam Keesey. Lambda Literary Award Nominee. ISBN 1-7344-014-0 10.95 paper.

Daughters of Darkness: Lesbian Vampire Stories, second edition, edited by Pam Keesey. ISBN: 1-57344-076-0   16.95 paper.

Vamps: An Illustrtated History of the Femme Fatale by Pam Keesey. ISBN: 1-57344-026-4 21.95.

Sons of Darkness: Tales of Men, Blood and Immortality, edited by Michael Rowe and Thomas S. Roche. Lambda Literary Award Nominee. ISBN: 1-57344-059-0 12.95 paper.

Women Who Run with the Werewolves: Tales of Blood, Lust and Metamorphosis, edited by Pam Keesey. Lambda Literary Award Nominee. ISBN: 1-57344-057-4 12.95 paper.

Erotica
Annie Sprinkle: Post Porn Modernist – My Twenty-Five Years as a Multimedia Whore by Annie Sprinkle. ISBN: 1-57344-039-6 $21.95 paper

Best Gay Erotica 1999. Selected and introduced by Felice Picano. Edited by Richard Labonté. ISBN: 1-57344-048-5. $14.95 paper.

Best Gay Erotica 1998, selected by Christopher Bram, edited by Richard Labonté. ISBN: 1-57344-031-0 14.95 paper.

Best Gay Erotica 1997, selected by Douglas Sadownick, edited by Richard Labonté. ISBN: 1-57344-067-1 14.95 paper.

Best Gay Erotica 1996, selected by Scott Heim, edited by Michael Ford. ISBN: 1-57344-052-3 12.95 paper.

Best Lesbian Erotica 1999. Selected and introduced by Chrystos. Edited by Tristan Taormino. ISBN: 1-57344-049-3. $14.95 paper.

Best Lesbian Erotica 1998, selected by Jenifer Levin, edited by Tristan Taormino. ISBN: 1-57344-032-9 14.95 paper.

The Leather Daddy and the Femme: An Erotic Novel by Carol Queen. ISBN: 1-57344-037-X. $14.00 paper.

Serious Pleasure: Lesbian Erotic Stories and Poetry, edited by the Sheba Collective. ISBN: 0-939416-45-X 9.95 paper.

Sex Guides
Good Sex: Real Stories from Real People, second edition, by Julia Hutton. ISBN: 1-57344-000-0 14.95 paper.

The New Good Vibrations Guide to Sex: Tips and techniques from America's favorite sex-toy store, second edition, by Cathy Winks and Anne Semans. ISBN: 1-57344-069-8 21.95 paper.

The Ultimate Guide to Anal Sex for Women by Tristan Taormino. ISBN: 1-57344-028-0 14.95 paper.

World Literature
A Forbidden Passion by Cristina Peri Rossi. ISBN: 0-939416-68-9 9.95 paper.

Half a Revolution: Contemporary Fiction by Russian Women, edited by Masha Gessen. ISBN 1-57344-006-X $12.95 paper.

Comix
Dyke Strippers: Lesbian Cartoonists A to Z, edited by Roz Warren. ISBN: 1-57344-008-6 16.95 paper.

Travel & Cooking

Betty and Pansy's Severe Queer Review of New York by Betty Pearl and Pansy. ISBN: 1-57344-070-1 10.95 paper.

Betty and Pansy's Severe Queer Review of San Francisco by Betty Pearl and Pansy. ISBN: 1-57344-056-6 10.95 paper.

Food for Life & Other Dish, edited by Lawrence Schimel. ISBN: 1-57344-061-2 14.95 paper.

Writer's Reference

Putting Out: The Essential Publishing Resource Guide For Gay and Lesbian Writers, fourth edition, by Edisol W. Dotson. ISBN: 1-57344-033-7 14.95 paper.

Cleis Press books are available at your favorite bookstore – or direct from us.
We welcome your order and will ship your books as quickly as possible.
Individual orders must be prepaid (U.S. dollars only).
Please add 15% shipping. (CA residents add 8.5% sales tax).
MasterCard and Visa orders:
include account number, exp. date, and signature.

How to Order

- **Phone:** 1-800-780-2279 or (415) 575-4700
  Monday - Friday, 9 am - 5 pm Pacific Standard Time
- **Fax:** (415) 575-4705
- **Mail: Cleis Press** P.O. Box 14684, San Francisco, California 94114
- **E-mail:** Cleis@aol.com